The Power of Purpose

The Power of Purpose

Find Meaning, Live Longer, Better

Second Edition

Richard J. Leider

BK

Berrett–Koehler Publishers, Inc.
San Francisco
a BK Life book

Berrett-Koehler Publishers, Inc.
1333 Broadway, Suite 1000
Oakland, CA 94612-1921
Tel: (510) 817-2277   Fax: (510) 817-2278   www.bkconnection.com

Ordering Information

Quantity sales. Special discounts are available on quantity purchases by corporations, associations, and others. For details, contact the "Special Sales Department" at the Berrett-Koehler address above.

Individual sales. Berrett-Koehler publications are available through most bookstores. They can also be ordered directly from Berrett-Koehler: Tel: (800) 929-2929; Fax: (802) 864-7626; www.bkconnection.com

Orders for college textbook/course adoption use. Please contact Berrett-Koehler: Tel: (800) 929-2929; Fax: (802) 864-7626.

Orders by U.S. trade bookstores and wholesalers. Please contact Ingram Publisher Services, Tel: (800) 509-4887; Fax: (800) 838-1149; E-mail: customer.service@ ingrampublisherservices.com; or visit www.ingrampublisherservices.com/Ordering for details about electronic ordering.

Berrett-Koehler and the BK logo are registered trademarks of Berrett-Koehler Publishers, Inc.

Printed in the United States of America

Berrett-Koehler books are printed on long-lasting acid-free paper. When it is available, we choose paper that has been manufactured by environmentally responsible processes. These may include using trees grown in sustainable forests, incorporating recycled paper, minimizing chlorine in bleaching, or recycling the energy produced at the paper mill.

Library of Congress Cataloging-in-Publication Data
Leider, Richard.
The power of purpose : find meaning, live longer, better / Richard J. Leider. — 2nd ed.
  p. cm.
Includes bibliographical references and index.
ISBN 978-1-60509-523-3 (pbk. : alk. paper)
1. Conduct of life.   2. Vocation.   3. Self-realization.   I. Title.
BF637.C5L44 2010
158--dc22
                                                                      2010005823

SECOND EDITION
20 19 18 17 16 15   10 9 8 7 6 5

Cover designer: Irene Morris Design
Text designer: Detta Penna
Copyeditor: Sandra Craig
Proofreader: Katherine Lee
Indexer: Joan Dickey
Cover photo: © Stuart / Fotolia

For Sally, Andrew, Greta, Austin, and Ethan:
you make it a meaningful life.

Contents

The Purpose Evolution

Your purpose.
Your aim or goal.
Your reason for being.
Your reason for getting up in the morning.

You may not have considered the first three items, but most of us have wondered about a reason to get up in the morning, at least occasionally. *The Power of Purpose,* Second Edition, is about that reason: to help you discover the purpose for your life.

What is purpose? Our purpose is an expression of the deepest dimension within us—of our central core or essence, where we have a profound sense of who we are, where we came from, and where we're going. Purpose, when it is clear, is the aim around which we structure our lives, a source of direction and energy, and the way the meaning of our lives is worked out in daily experience. You have a purpose no matter what age you are, how healthy you are, or what your economic or social situation is. Your purpose is the reason you were born, and it can be what gets you out of bed in the morning.

Power is the other key word in the book's title that needs attention. *Webster's Dictionary* defines power as the "ability to do, act, or produce." Only certain kinds of purpose have the potential to be empowering, so being deliberate about identifying our purpose is essential. What determines the power in purpose, ultimately, is the worthiness of the focus. Having purpose that provides real power requires a goal outside ourselves. Only when our focus—our purpose—is larger than ourselves can meaning be deeply savored and long lasting, not just a goal completed and then forgotten.

At our very core we need to matter. We need evidence to believe that we are good people and are evolving—becoming the best we can be. Naming our purpose helps us satisfy a basic need that we're being used for a purpose that we recognize as a worthy one.

Many of us say we don't have enough time to take care of our careers and our lives. Then before we know it, we're right! We are so busy trying to survive in an increasingly complex world that we don't have time to notice time passing. We do many things to answer the question Why do I get up in the morning? However, our busyness can also be a way of avoiding the question. In addition, it is an anxious way of living that can lead to unease and psychological and physical problems. And finally, we might end up asking, What have I done with my life?

Find Meaning. Live Longer, Better

There is a better way. Having a reason to get up in the morning is associated in numerous scientific studies with better mental and physical health and greater longevity. Purpose can add not only years to your life but also life to your years!

If you are looking for a reason to get up in the morning or asking questions such as these, this book is for you:

- I feel that I've missed my calling in life. How do I find it?

- I've successfully reached midlife. Is that all there is? What's next?

- I've been growing spiritually. How do I connect my spiritual growth with my work?

- I'm in a major transition (graduation, marriage, new job or job loss, divorce, illness, death of a loved one). How do I find meaning and direction?

- I have enough outer success. How do I find inner fulfillment?

This book was developed by interviewing older adults (over the age of sixty-five) about such deep questions, then combining their wisdom with my studies in the fields of adult development and counseling psychology. Specifically, I asked a cross-section of older adults this question: "If you could live your life over again, what would you do differently?"

Three themes wove their way through all the interviews. The respondents consistently said they would

- Be more reflective.

- Be more courageous.

- Be clear earlier about purpose.

From these interviews, I concluded that purpose naturally resides deep inside the human soul. All people seem to have a natural desire and capacity to contribute somehow to life.

Each of us wants to leave footprints. And each of us has a unique purpose. Each is an experiment of one. We can learn from but not adopt the purpose of another person but must uncover our own. Each of us is on a quest to find our purpose, whether we are consciously pursuing the quest or are vaguely aware that something is missing.

Throughout history, humans have sought to make sense of their lives, searching for meaning through prayer, retreat, art, music, nature, community, gratitude, forgiveness, and multiple other ways. Traditionally, purpose was connected with the spiritual aspect of people's lives, and healers, priests, and shamans were the ministers who helped people connect with the sacred to restore bodies and souls to health and wholeness. Now science is increasingly validating what people have known all along: that purpose is essential. When it comes to life's inevitable breakdowns, purpose can provide a breakthrough. Purpose can give us the will to live. Without purpose, we can die. With purpose, we can live in dignity and compassion. Purpose dramatically affects our longevity and well-being, and it is the one thing that cannot be taken from us.

The twenty-first century shift to an accelerated, global, technology-driven world is a major transformation. Such periods tend to spotlight what does not change—what remains constant and nonnegotiable in our lives. Purpose is one of those constants. People of all ages are seeking a new perspective on how they fit into this evolving world. We are challenged to find relevant answers to the age-old questions of purpose and meaning. In this century, purpose has the marks of a movement—an inner-directed revolution. We could say that we are living in the purpose age.

In addition, many of us have come to acknowledge publicly what we privately knew all along: that surviving adolescence and early adulthood did not ensure a tranquil, jolt-free passage through the rest of our careers and lives. We change; our priorities and values shift; confidence grows, dissolves into doubt, returns; relationships evolve, break apart, reform; careers and lifestyles lose energy or take on new interest—all forming a complex life cycle. Thus, purpose is not discovered once and then we are done with it. It is reexamined at various points throughout the life cycle, typically during crises and major life transitions.

Welcome to the Second Edition

I chose to write this book because of my deep personal belief that we live in an evolving spiritual world and that every individual in this world has unique gifts and a purpose to use those gifts to contribute value to the world.

This book builds on earlier editions of *The Power of Purpose,* expanding and deepening the conversation. It is based on twenty-five years of experiences with people of all ages who were engaged in the purpose quest. New stories about purpose have been added, and other material has been updated. In addition, the Resources at the back of the book have been updated for the many people who asked me how to use the book in seminars, classes, book clubs, and spiritual or study groups.

The book is organized in a way that makes sense to me, but everyone has different needs and interests, so you should feel free to follow any order you want to.

I believe that spirit touches and moves our lives through the evolution of purpose. That is my starting point for helping people to uncover their purpose. In a pluralistic society, not everyone will agree with that starting point. That's all right. Let me be clear, however, that my objective is not intended to express a religious point of view or to exclude people who don't believe as I do. Instead, this starting point is the very reason for my acceptance of the many differences among people. Because of my starting point, I believe that each person has a spiritual reason for being and that our world is incomplete until each one uncovers her or his purpose.

I hope that you will uncover your purpose—if I have found mine, this book will be a catalyst for finding yours.

Richard J. Leider
Minneapolis, Minnesota

Part I

The Meaning of Purpose

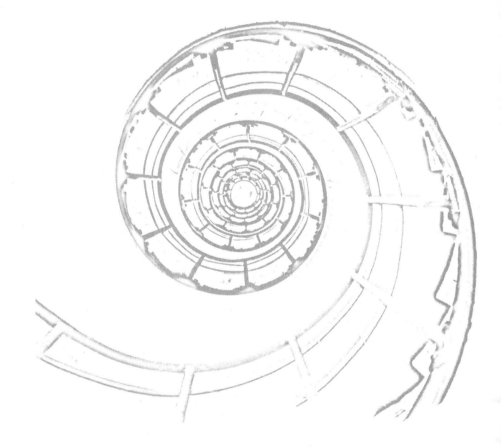

Chapter 1

The Purpose Moment

I was just trying to get home from work.

Rosa Parks

Purpose is fundamental to human life. It is what makes us human. Purpose is not only what makes us human, it is the one thing that cannot be taken from us. Purpose gives us the will to live or to persevere. It gives us a reason to get up in the morning. Purpose gives us courage.

Most of us want to know that there is a purpose to life—that our being here does mean something and that what we do matters. Most of us want our lives to matter, and we want to live courageously.

Purpose is one of the chief requisites for courage in life. A constant in the lives of people who experience a sense of courage is the "purpose moment"—moments of meaning. This chapter shows the importance of purpose moments to the purpose quest and helps you to recognize and create such moments in your own life.

The Power of a Purpose Moment

Rosa Parks had a purpose moment that ultimately changed a nation. She was arrested for refusing to give up her bus seat to a white passenger in Montgomery, Alabama, on December 1, 1955. This single act of courage sparked a bus boycott that led to the integration of Alabama's bus system and paved the way for the civil rights movement in the United States.

The search for dignity is basic to us all. However, we often become deeply concerned about it only when some crisis forces us to confront it—an arrest, an illness, a death, a divorce, or a loss of job. We take life for granted until a crisis wakes us up and forces us to ask the big questions. Crisis is a catalyst for purpose moments. And purpose moments bring us face to face with the big questions, such as What am I meant to do here?

Flight 427 was scheduled to depart Chicago's O'Hare Airport at 4:50 p.m. on a hectic Friday afternoon. Bill was on his way to Pittsburgh to attend his first meeting of the executive committee of a college board of trustees. Just before flight time, above the din of a busy O'Hare, Bill heard a page that asked him to check with the nearest gate agent. He was instructed to call his office immediately, where he learned that his meeting had been canceled—the first such cancellation in eleven years!

Shortly before Flight 427 was to begin boarding, Bill turned in his boarding pass and made a quick exit to another concourse, where his assistant, Nancy, had booked him on a flight back to his hometown of Atlanta. When he called his wife, Valerie, on his cell phone from his car on the way home, he was greeted by an outburst of tears and raw emotion. "Bill," she sobbed, "you haven't heard! The plane you were supposed to be on to Pittsburgh crashed short of the airport and no one survived."

Bill was stunned. Of that purpose moment on the freeway, he said, "There was only this amazing calm, a sense of peace that settled over me and affirmed that God was holding me in the palm of His hand." He arrived home to tears of joy and hugs that didn't want to quit, while the television brought the bitter details of Flight 427 into their living room. Bill reflects, "I know my reprieve is temporary. My life has been extended for now."

Bill believes that God had something more to accomplish through his life. On Monday after his narrow escape, he got a hint of what that purpose might be. At his insurance agency, where he was managing director, he was besieged by friends, staff, and agents, all expressing gratitude for his role in their lives. Bill was already the leader of one of the largest, most successful insurance agencies in the country, but at that moment he realized that his true purpose, from here on, was to "grow values-driven people." That became the mission of his life and agency. Bill no longer postponed those critical coaching conversations but focused his newly precious time on coaching people to live in alignment with their purpose.

What Is a Life Purpose?

Our well-being and quality of life depend on finding greater wholeness in life. The words *health, heal, whole,* and *holy* all derive from the same root. This reveals the obvious fact that to grow whole is not just a challenge of money and health but a challenge of meaning as well.

Having a purpose in life—a clear reason to get up in the morning—is essential to growing whole. Imagine that you've decided to conduct your own personal survey by asking a handful of your friends, What is a life purpose? What do you guess the most common answer might be? Would it be similar to your own response or quite different?

At first glance, it might seem like the answer to the question is so obvious that it's a waste of your time to even ask it. Don't be fooled, however. There is wisdom in revisiting the questions that we think we already know how to answer. Our answers change at different phases of our lives and with changing life circumstances.

I've dedicated my professional life to exploring that single question. Consequently, I've had the privilege of asking thousands of people that question and many others. I've discovered that the majority of people answer the question What is a life purpose? in a very similar way. They may use different words, but the common thread weaving through their responses is this: "A life purpose is what I'm meant to do and be while I'm here on the earth."

Purpose Is What Makes Us Human

So, what is your individual purpose? Whether we explore this question publicly or privately, it is vital to our health, healing, wholeness, and our holiness that we do examine the question. Because what ultimately shape our lives are the questions we ask, fail to ask, or never dream of asking. It is our questions that shape our humanity.

If we had to name what makes life worth living, what gives it meaning and purpose, most of us would probably say it's the people we love. Relationships, along with work, are the core differences in quality of life at all ages. Whom we love and how we love them are in a way the core reasons we get up in the morning.

Yet the number-one issue in many people's lives today is loneliness. A sense of aloneness—a strong feeling of isolation or going it alone—affects almost half of us. We complain that we either want more time for friends or would like to have more true friends, versus acquaintances, because busy lives can result in an abundance of acquaintances and a poverty of true friends.

We can easily fill our lives with busyness. There is always more to be done, always a way to keep from staring into the mirror. If we're not careful, we can begin to mistake our busyness for meaning, turning our lives into a checklist of to-dos that can occupy all the waking hours of our days and leave us breathless, with our feeling of friendship left incomplete.

And always there is more to do. Our to-do lists will outlive us. The labors of our lives will be endless. For every person who summons up the focus and energy to step out on the purpose quest, there are many more who plod on, waiting—waiting for some magical, easy solution to their quest, waiting for a sign.

Discovering What Matters

The Met Life Mature Market Institute (MMI) applied sophisticated market research to the philosophical question of purpose. The MMI team worked closely with me and used my purpose work as a foundation for the purpose model in this study. The study, titled Discovering What Matters, explored with a researcher's eye for precision the way people prioritize their lives as they face challenges. This marriage of measurement to meaning produced unique, measurable evidence about the role purpose plays in people's lives. It revealed that regardless of age, gender, financial status, or life phase, the majority of people assign the most importance to meaning-related activities and, above all else, spending time with friends and family.

People with a sense of purpose in their lives were more likely to report being "happy" and to describe themselves as living the "good life." Having a sense of purpose was related to possessing both a "focus" on essential things today, and a "vision" of the future they wanted to enjoy.

The study showed that the concept of purpose, even the word itself, is something held in high regard by many, perhaps even most people. Some described purpose as giving them a general direction for their lives, while others even went so far as to allow it to prioritize the key choices required in their day-to-day living. And yet, many of the respondents might have found it difficult to honestly point to how they would use purpose in the daily choices they make.

But is purpose merely an esoteric idea that is nice to have, or a more powerful universal concept? Responses revealed that purpose was the differentiator between those who reported living the "good life" and those not living the good life. Eighty-four percent of those who felt their lives had purpose reported that they were living the good life.

A "Build-Your-Own" trade-off exercise was used to assess people's expectations of what their lives would be like with respect to activities five years in the future. They were given a set number of "life points" to distribute among a range of activities in four categories: money, medicine, meaning, and place. Consistent with results from other parts of the study, respondents across all age groups allocated the most life points to meaning-related activities—that is, being with friends and family—with older respondents (aged sixty-five to seventy-four) focusing the most time on meaning-related activities.

It is clear from this research that mature adults are driven by the pursuit of meaning and purpose in their lives, and that the older people are, the more important living with meaning and purpose becomes. While there are certainly some differences among age, income, and asset levels, the consistent message from this research is that the circumstances that truly bring a sense of contentment, happiness, and satisfaction to life are fairly universal.[1]

Everyone Else Has a Purpose. So What's Mine?

An entertaining evocation of this purpose research is the musical *Avenue Q*, which is the twenty-first longest-running show in Broadway history and has won several Tony Awards, including the award for best musical. The show has also spawned other productions around the globe, including the one I experienced at the Gielgud Theatre in London.

The show is largely inspired by (and is in the style of) *Sesame Street*. Most of the characters in the show are puppets operated by actors onstage; the set depicts several tenements on a rundown street in an outer borough of New York City. However, the characters are in their twenties and thirties and face adult problems instead of those faced by preschoolers, thus making the show more suited for the adults who grew up with *Sesame Street*. A recurring theme is the central character's search for his elusive "purpose."

I sat enthralled as the song "Purpose" was sung. The core message—"Everyone else has a purpose. So, what's mine?"—brought forth murmurs from the strangers sitting around me, as they chuckled over the lyrics, such as "Purpose—it's the little flame that lights a fire under your ass. / Purpose, it's like driving a car with a full tank of gas," and others. I left the theater that night feeling affirmed that purpose had truly arrived in the public discourse. From shows in London and Las Vegas, from youngsters and oldsters, the ever-elusive-purpose-in-life theme was finally on the marquee. *Avenue Q* was a purpose moment for me.

It is often a purpose moment that awakens us to our gifts and passions. Benjamin Jackson was running in a local 10K weekend race in which a number of wheelchair athletes were also participating. A postrace conversation with one of these athletes led Ben to an awareness of the challenges they faced in their normal day-to-day activities. Soon he explored the realities of wheelchair life at the college he was attending and at his mother's workplace. He began writing letters and lobbying his school's administration to provide funds for greater accessibility to athletics for students with disabilities. Ben went on to study architecture and now consults with organizations on making their buildings more accessible to people with physical challenges. Fulfilling work began with a purpose moment following a 10K race, and today it serves as Ben's calling.

Purpose helps us understand what is core to our life, what we care about in our actual day-to-day living. Our world suddenly makes sense to us.

The Purpose Game

There are purpose moments that we could all take advantage of by extending ourselves into the world. When you want to give yourself a lift, you can play the "purpose game."

Here's how the game is played. Look around, wherever you happen to be, and see what or who needs your touch. For example, while driving, maybe you could let other cars in front of you while driving all the way to your destination. Another possibility is to tell your spouse or a significant other a new reason he or she is important to you. Or you could buy coffee for a friend for no reason; create an end-of-day celebration because you lived this day; get up early to write an e mail or handwritten note of gratitude to someone.

The important idea is to play consciously in life, giving your gifts or serving others. You want to do little things that make you feel on purpose. We often put a lot of energy into doing the big things, but we want to feel on purpose "all" the moments of life. There are "purpose moments" everywhere, every day that we could fill up with ourselves. When we are watching, ready to play the purpose game, the possibilities are endless.

Make a list of purpose moments you could play tomorrow that would be unexpected and make you feel good. What are your favorite games of purpose?

A Purpose Moment That Changed Me

One person who had a profound purpose-moment effect on my life was Richard Reusch, my college advisor. To this day, I can cite material from his lectures verbatim. Dr. Reusch required students to pick up their exams in his office so he could talk with each one. More than test grades were the subject of discussions in his office, however. At the end of my first semester at Gustavus Adolphus College, in danger of flunking out, I went to talk to Dr. Reusch before final exams. I can still smell the pipe smoke and picture his office, where he was surrounded by African artifacts collected in his forty years of work as the "Maasai missionary" in Tanzania.

"I'm really lost," I told him. "I want to stay here, but I've really screwed up my life. What should I do?"

Dr. Reusch didn't ask about my courses but simply asked me to tell him something about myself. "About myself?" No other professor had ever asked me that! A magical hour later, I left his office with a vision for what I wanted in school and in life. Somehow, Dr. Reusch made the hour almost a spiritual experience, and I knew something special was intended for my life.

Twenty years later I traveled to Tanzania and climbed Mount Kilimanjaro. I was astonished to learn that the crater at the summit is named Reusch Crater. Dr. Reusch climbed Mount Kilimanjaro sixty-five times, helped to establish its exact altitude, and discovered the crater now officially named after him. He knew twenty languages, and he wrote books on religion, history, and geography in German, English, and Swahili.

Richard Reusch came to Minnesota and taught church history, comparative religion, and fencing at Gustavus Adolphus. His archive files are stuffed with letters of appreciation from young people, from parents of students, and from Maasai leaders in Tanzania, who said, "Come, please, and help us again."

He concluded his ministry, or service, at St. John's Church at Stacy, Minnesota, of which he still was the pastor when he died. Two weeks previously, he had announced his resignation date. That date became the occasion of his funeral.

Dr. Reusch used to say that a miracle occurred when a need and a solution converged. That day in his office I witnessed a miracle, thanks to a life memorably lived. He was one of the most purposeful people I have ever crossed paths with.

Purpose is the recognition of the purpose moments in life and the courage to choose a life that is aligned with that purpose. Purpose defines our contribution to life, moment to moment. It may find expression through family, community, relationship, work, and spiritual activities. We receive from life what we give, and in the process we understand more of what it means to "show up in the moment."

Look ahead. How old do you think you'll live to be? Imagine you're that age. As you look back on your life, what would you like to be able to say is your legacy? How did you become the person you were destined to be? What might you do to create purpose moments so that you can look back over your life with no regrets?

Chapter 2

The Purpose Quest

Service is the rent we pay for living. It is the very purpose of life, and not something you do in your spare time.

Marian Wright Edelman

Viktor Frankl, Holocaust survivor, therapist, and author of *Man's Search for Meaning,* notes that many of us are questioning life, and suggests instead, "Let life question you!" We ask: What has life done for me? Will things go my way today? What's in it for me? However, there is a more profound wisdom in reversing the questioning and letting life question us. An openness to being questioned by life is a way to uncover our purpose.

It is often in the midst of profound purpose moments that we pull back from the entanglements of daily survival and let life question us. The benefit of a crisis is often the letting go of petty concerns, conflicts, and the need for control and the realization that life is short and every moment precious.

Cancer therapists Carl and Stephanie Simonton give their patients this advice:

> You must stop and reassess your priorities and values. You must be willing to be yourself, not what people want you to be because you think that is the only way you can get love. You can no longer be dishonest. You are now at a point where, if you truly want to live, you have to be who you are.[2]

Could there be any better advice for us?

Whenever we are confronted with a purpose moment, such as cancer or a fate that is unavoidable, we are given the choice to let life question us. What matters is the attitude we take toward the situation. This chapter will help you learn to let life question you.

Marathon of Hope

A sense of purpose is rarely handed to us. We get it by choosing it, by choosing to say, "Yes, I matter; I want my life to matter." Because a sense of purpose comes from within, only we know if we have it. Only we are aware if something in our life makes us want to get up in the morning.

Terry Fox[3] is a clear example. For this young Canadian, the necessity to discover his purpose was thrust upon him early in life. Two days after his eighteenth birthday, Terry learned he had a cancerous tumor in his right knee. His leg would have to be amputated immediately because the cancer could spread through the rest of his body. Suddenly, life was tentative, no longer to be taken for granted. Despite the shock and the speed with which Terry's life had changed, he spent little time in the trap of self-pity. Within the confines of his hospital room, Terry detected a purpose moment, his personal reason to live.

Many of us will be forced to reflect upon the reason for our existence when we experience severe crises. But as Terry Fox put it, "You don't have to do like I did—wait until you lose a leg or get some awful disease—before you can take the time to find out what kind of stuff you're made of. Start now. Anybody can."

Two weeks after his surgery, Terry began chemotherapy. The cancer clinic and the painful treatments were a reminder to Terry that almost half of all cancer patients never recover. He began to detect what he cared deeply about; what moved him. He decided to do something for the people who were still in the hospital. Terry began to uncover a new sense of purpose, which crystallized into a specific project: he would run all the way across Canada to raise one million dollars to fight cancer and would give the money to the Canadian Cancer Society.

The power of purpose had transformed an average athlete into a person who ran a marathon a day for five months with an artificial leg! After completing three-fifths of the journey across Canada, Terry Fox had to leave his Marathon of Hope. He never finished because the cancer had spread to his lungs. But by the time of his death, one year later, he had surpassed his goal. He had raised many millions of dollars and had inspired hundreds of thousands of people. Life questioned Terry and he answered.

Terry Fox symbolized what most of us want to believe
—that there is purpose to life, that our being here does
mean something, that what we do does matter. The sheer
determination of one individual can turn a seemingly mediocre
idea into a stunning success. The lesson for us is that behind
the creation of any great deed is at least one individual who
was consumed by a purpose to make a difference. And the
only place we can find this kind of motivation is within.

Purpose Myths

If you feel inclined to dismiss Terry Fox's story as bigger than
life with no practical application for your own purpose quest,
you may be subscribing to some commonly held myths about
purpose.

It's not just the high achievers but people who achieve
less dramatic successes as well—all the people in this
book—who have to overcome their self-imposed doubts and
other obstacles to get started when they discover what moves
them. The following are four common myths that may block
us from intentionally moving ahead toward our purpose. As
you read each one, ask yourself, Do I believe this?

Myth 1: To have purpose means I must do something
completely original.

> *Reality:* Can you think of anything that is totally new?
> Almost every idea or creation is an extension or synthesis
> of previous ideas. New scientific breakthroughs are built
> on existing fundamental truths, often as the result of
> reorganizing or reapplying old concepts. As we uncover

our purpose, we often need to accept this fact: that at
the heart, most new ideas result from borrowing, adding,
combining, or modifying old ones. Like runners in a
relay race, we simply carry the baton another leg of the
race.

Action: The paradox of purpose is that in order to address
new solutions to problems, we must first familiarize
ourselves with the ideas of others to form a base for
launching our own ideas. Gather as much information as
you can (realizing that you'll never have enough). Make a
decision. Get on with the business of living on purpose.

Myth 2: Only a few special people have true purpose in their
lives.

Reality: This is the most commonly rationalized of all
myths. There is no denying that often we have relied on
saints, sages, and experts to solve many of our problems.
However, history is filled with great contributions made
by ordinary people who had virtually no expertise in
the areas where they made their mark. In fact, being a
novice is often an asset because we aren't hemmed in by
traditional ways of viewing a situation.

Action: Purpose appears and is successful in proportion
to the energies we expend rather than to our degree of
expertise. It's the passion to make a difference that counts
most, so we must carefully tend our passion.

Myth 3: True purpose comes as inspiration or revelation. Until
that time comes, I might as well keep plodding ahead.

Reality: The "pop-in" theory of motivation would have us believe that creative ideas and new directions are flashes of brilliance that suddenly appear to the fortunate: purpose descends on the lucky few. If we believe that, nothing will happen for sure! Any successful person can attest to the absurdity of waiting to be inspired.

Action: Inspiration comes to those who seek it. First we begin, then purpose moments appear.

Myth 4: Purpose is nice, but impractical. I need money!

Reality: Many times we become so caught in day-to-day survival activity that we lose sight of what we're doing, and our activity becomes a false end in itself rather than a means to an end. Henry David Thoreau put it bluntly: "It isn't enough to be busy. Ants are busy." The question we should ask ourselves is What are we busy about?

"Gee, I'd love to get involved, but who's got the time? I have a spouse, job, children, and financial commitments. How on earth can you expect me to find the time?" Sound familiar? For most of us, time is indeed the bigger barrier. But waiting until we have the time is as futile as trying to save money by putting away what we don't happen to spend.

Action: The only way to commit time to purpose is to steal it from some other activity. This is what the power of purpose is all about—aligning our energies around our true priorities.

Finding Goals and Something Else

Terry Fox had a direct impact on my own life. While camping around the perimeter of Lake Superior, I came upon Terry Fox running just outside of Thunder Bay, Ontario. Sandwiched between the flashing red lights of a highway patrol car and the van with a Marathon of Hope banner on its side was Terry Fox—with a look in his eyes that is etched indelibly in my mind. That look of determination was the power of purpose in action. The unexpected meeting planted the seed that led to the writing of this book.

He challenged me with that look. He made me ask, "What am I trying to do with my life?"

Ever since I was a child, I've had an intense curiosity about what motivates people. I've always felt convinced that there could be more to my life if only I could find it. Tempted by the glowing promises of self-help books, I read them all, and they all said, "The first step is to decide what your goals in life are." So I sat down cheerfully one day with pencil in hand to jot down my goals. They didn't come!

The self-help books had suggested that I should want some specific goals—for example, to be successful, to earn a certain amount of money. But none of these goals moved me. I was unable to find the clear passion that Terry Fox had, that would make my goals meaningful. I was beginning to question whether there might be something wrong with me.

Whenever I did manage to commit myself to a goal, I found I achieved more success than I ever expected, but the results never brought me the fulfillment the books promised. I had never been able to find in one of those goals a meaningful focus for my life. On one day, a certain goal would be important; on another day, a different goal would capture my fancy. I rarely committed myself to anything passionately. I wanted to work for a purpose, not just for a living or for one goal after another.

Embracing Purpose Before Goals

In describing people like Terry Fox, who have uncovered a sense of purpose, I once felt a certain amount of uneasiness. I didn't want to describe a goal that seemed so unrealistic, so ideal. Purpose had always meant goals to me, but Terry Fox got me thinking again. I started to realize that goals were not the same as purpose, and that I needed to embrace a purpose before I selected my goals. I began again, this time to shape a purpose for my life. And it was no longer the shaping of life to fit my ego-driven goals but rather the gradual detecting of a purpose outside myself.

Terry Fox showed the true joy I sought for my own life. He was alive! I realized that it is not our specific goals that create this aliveness; it is the sense of purpose with which we embrace the goals.

People with a sense of purpose have learned to let life question them and have moved the focus of their attention and concern away from themselves to others.

Purpose, then, is not a job or a role or a goal. It is the belief that our lives, our part in the whole of things, truly matters. Having a profound sense of who we are, where we came from, and where we're going, we choose to believe that mattering matters. It is thus a mindset—a choice. It is first and foremost the choice to choose "life" despite the circumstances we find ourselves in. It is the choice to bring who we are—our gifts and energies—to whatever we are doing. Purpose is a cradle-to-grave, 24/7, moment-to-moment choice in our daily lives.

One purpose in life is not more important than another. There is purpose whenever we use our gifts and talents to respond to something we believe in.

You Were Not Born for Nothing

It may or may not be a new idea that you were born for a reason, for some purpose. If you have never considered the idea that you have a life purpose, now is the time to tell your mind that you're going to look at life in a new way for a while. You might even question your own skepticism because you are now curious about this notion that you were born for a reason.

You may be one of the many who has always felt inside that there is some meaning to your life, and you would be very happy to live with a purpose if only you could find it.

Whatever your present position is about purpose, relax. There is a place deep inside you that is yearning to believe that you were born for something.

Thinking Larger

The reason many people have difficulty in uncovering their life purpose is because they do not see themselves as large enough. Thinking larger about yourself means coming to terms with the fact that, whether you concur or not, it makes a difference that *you* are living this life. You may never have experienced a large purpose moment like Terry Fox did, but still it makes a difference that you are alive, living this moment on this earth. Thinking large simply means that you have embraced the power of purpose—that you realize that you contribute something special.

It's About Uncovering Something You Already Have

The great thing about your life purpose is that you already have it, and you already know many things about it. You're not going to uncover some unsuspected thing about yourself that you could never do.

Uncovering your life purpose is really a process of self-discovery and self-acceptance. It may be, as it is for many people, that you have so discounted your gifts that you have lost sight of your most valuable assets. You may believe that only special people, like Terry Fox, can find and have a purpose, and you have never considered yourself special.

Whatever your thoughts might have been, now you are thinking about yourself in a new way. You acknowledge that something about you is unique, special. You are aware that your life is as significant as anyone else's, and you intend to act on that fact. You can choose how you want to live, work, and relate. It is not a surprise, now that you want to express the best of yourself.

When you are acting on your life purpose, you claim your power and feel that people need you and appreciate your gifts. Take time to notice the times when you feel especially engaged in life. How can you create more of those times?

Chapter 3

The Purpose Spiral

We are all on a spiral path. No growth takes place in a straight line. There will be setbacks along the way. . . . There will be shadows, but they will be balanced by patches of light. . . . Awareness of the pattern is all you need to sustain you along the way.

Kristin Zambucka

All life is a spiral of change, a continuous graceful curve toward purpose. There is a definite pattern to it all, and we spend our whole lives seeking that pattern by living with different questions at each age and phase. Searching for the pattern is the heart of our human quest. If we're aware of that pattern, and our place in it, we can identify the best choices to sustain us along the way.

Most of us find that our purpose evolves as experiences change over our lifetime. A new sense of purpose may be triggered when we reach a particular age, by a crisis, or by a natural, ongoing discovery of who we are.

Asking new questions as we age is part of the quest for purpose. This chapter will help you detect the spiral pattern of your own life and recognize your current question.

The Spiral

If living on purpose sounds like an impractical order, think about a spiral. The *Random House Unabridged Dictionary of the English Language* defines a spiral as "running continually around a fixed point or center while constantly receding from or approaching it." The spiral projects the image of a continuity that coils in one plane around one particular center, like the spiral staircase on this book's cover. There is a clear analogy between the path of purpose and the pattern of a spiral staircase: each has a basic center of orientation that provides a coherent pattern. Think of your life as a spiral staircase, with many steps behind you and many ahead.

The spiral is a natural pattern for discovering our purpose in today's world. As we, too, move through different phases, our purpose evolves. The old phases feel cramped and lack room to stretch and breathe. We outgrow people, places, and passions. We move on to new phases to make way for the new growth to emerge.

As Pat Murphy and William Neill see it in their book *By Nature's Design*: "Life more often than not does not draw straight lines. The world is filled with graceful curves—from the elegant spiral in the heart of the nautilus shell to the twisting double helix of DNA that codes for the nautilus' growth."[4]

For Each Phase of Life, a Particular Question

We do not remain children forever but rather move through various phases toward wisdom and maturity. As we move through each stage of our own pattern of growth, we naturally look in different directions and ask different questions. Each phase of our life has its own special question, and the way we answer the questions determines our pattern.

Discovering our pattern is what it means to be human. Life is a continuous spiral of questions to be answered and lessons to be learned. We grow through phases of progressive awakenings that involve physical, mental, emotional, and spiritual insights.

If you look back and examine the past phases of your life, each contained a natural yet core question. And as you lived in the core questions, they taught you the essential truths of life and showed you new questions.

The secret to a fully alive life is learning how to reframe our life questions over and over, letting go of what is no longer relevant, and taking on new questions guided by our evolving maturity. Each phase is naturally important as a basis for further growth.

Life As an Improvisatory Art

Each transition to a new phase of purpose is accompanied by a crisis of uncertainty, a chaotic period of time in which we are organizing ourselves around a new core question. In fact, our phases may never seem quite settled, may not follow a plan or outline that we might have imagined or expected. Perhaps rather than using words such as *developments, stages,* or *phases,* we might consider another word: *improvisations.*

Anthropologist Mary Catherine Bateson observed in her book *Composing a Life* that the adult years are not linear but fluid and even disjointed. She wrote:

> The model of an ordinary successful life that is held up for young people is one of early decision and commitment, often to an educational preparation that launches a single rising trajectory. . . . Many of societies' casualties are men and women who assumed they had chosen a path in life and found that it disappeared in the underbrush.[5]

Bateson called adult life "an improvisatory art, about the ways we combine familiar and unfamiliar components in response to new situations."

One reason for the improvisatory nature of life phases now may be that a growing number of people are expecting their work to provide daily meaning as well as their daily bread. They want work that integrates their unique gifts and talents with the practical realities of surviving and making a living.

After graduating from college, my son, Andrew Leider, like many young people, wanted both meaning and money. "What's your purpose?" I asked Andrew over coffee one morning. He quickly responded, "To make my way in the world without losing myself!"

Andrew never intended to live what he called a "tract life" after college. He was not looking for what he'd do for the next forty years. While many of his friends were becoming lawyers, doctors, ministers, and businesspeople, he was enjoying a different quest and different questions. His core question was, "What am I willing to trade my time for without compromising my values?"

Because of his passion for adventure, he gravitated to work for the wilderness-based Outward Bound schools. The purpose of Outward Bound is to conduct safe, adventure-based programs structured to inspire self-esteem, self-reliance, concern for others, and care for the environment. As an Outward Bound instructor, Andrew studied intensely and uncovered a natural gift for designing, directing, and leading wilderness courses. He found that "Outward Bound fulfills my personality for the predictable future. Although I'm not making much money, I am able to survive nicely and integrate who I am with what I do."

Outward Bound ran its natural course for Andrew. After ten years, a new growth phase was coming within reach, and it was time to move on. The next phase combined his Somatic Coach Certification with both his management and wilderness leadership skills. As executive director of Montana Yellowstone Expeditions, he is able to follow a deeper call to help youth find their way in the world.

The magic of this work for Andrew is that it is a place that consciously supports the integration of his work and his life. It gives him the opportunity to improvise—to bring his whole self to work and to experience the integrity of working without compromising his values.

The late management consultant Peter Drucker described career choices: "The probability that the first choice you make is right for you is roughly one in a million. If you decide that your first choice was the right one, chances are you are just plain lazy."[6] This should not be discouraging because everything we do builds toward our next life phase and the evolution of our purpose. Rarely do we have wasted work, though at the time it might seem that way. We're always growing and mastering life's lessons—even hard-to-recognize ones—that move us forward on purpose.

We're all challenged to shape and create the specific and unique way we are going to do the work we are called to do. It takes resolve to make what we do reflect who we are. Yet we are often not encouraged to do that. From early childhood, we are taught to behave in ways that fit the purposes of others. As children, we are naturally open yet dependent on the lead set by others. Following the lead of our parents, peers, teachers, and others brings approval. Sooner or later, we realize it is easier to base our choices on what is expected of us rather than on what is meaningful to us. Sometimes we become so dependent on these external standards that we no longer know what we truly need or want.

Instead of improvising and continuing to take risks on our spiral journey, many of us stop and wait for something to happen. We wait for the grand opportunity, when our full gifts and talents will be unleashed and used, not committing ourselves to anything until everything is right. Waiting by its very nature traps us in a way of living that makes our life feel superficial and disappointing. We become stalled on our purpose spiral.

If we do not discover our purpose, then a large portion of each day is spent doing something we might not truly care about and would rather not be doing. We may spend so much of our lives waiting that we miss the true joy of purposeful living and remain unfulfilled. The spiral will end. Death will claim us, and we will not have had more than a moment of contentment.

Purpose Is Immortal

One of the requirements of discovering our calling is to come face to face with the sacred, mysterious part of ourselves. To do that we must make friends with death. Living and working on purpose means eventually facing squarely the question of mortality.

Mary Foley's life spiral was ended before she was able to complete her journey. Mary believed deeply in human potential, and she believed in herself. As corporate manager of health services for a major manufacturing company, Mary was one of those rare mentors who consistently held positive expectations of people and encouraged them not to settle for less than their higher purpose. Her purpose was "to be a positive influence on the lives of women and children." Mentoring other women in her field was the work she loved. By believing in the dreams of other young professional women, Mary uncovered her gifts, uncovered her passions, and shared her own struggles and questions.

Mary frequently checked on what people were reading, talked about what she was reading, and often recommended or gave books to others. She discovered an earlier edition of this book and gave it to many people. She inquired and was genuinely interested in people's core questions, especially around purpose.

Tragically, Mary was murdered. Her purpose was snuffed out at an early age. Mary had helped many young women express their dreams. She played her role in creating the kind of world she dreamed of. An organization called the Friends of Mary Foley keeps her purpose alive in the community. Every year since her death, a group of her friends get together on her birthday to celebrate and toast her life. Each year they raise money and resources for a cause that aligns with Mary's purpose. One of her friends said, "She lived with more purpose than most anyone I have known." Her purpose is immortal.

Core Questions

Purpose helps us live in the questions that are meaningful and life enhancing. Purpose provides the courage to overcome the stressful challenges that come with each phase of life. In childhood we ask, Who am I? In adolescence, the question becomes What do I want to be when I grow up? In young adulthood we want to know What is my calling? In "middlessence" we mull over What's calling me next? In young older adulthood, the question becomes How do I grow whole, not old? In elderhood we ask, What's my legacy?

If we live and answer these core questions, our answers will be satisfying when we look back over our lives and ask such questions as Was it worth it? and Did my life matter? We will feel that our time here was well spent, that our legacy is a positive one. In contrast, when we have no purpose, we wander directionless through life, fail to realize our full potential, and sometimes look back with despair over wasted time and opportunities.

Viktor Frankl, the Jewish psychiatrist who survived the horrors of the Nazi concentration camps, taught me the importance of finding purpose and meaning. He claimed that it was the key to survival when his choices were few and the future seemed hopeless. He and other prisoners who maintained a sense of meaning or purpose in life were the ones who were able to transcend the brutal and desperate circumstances of the

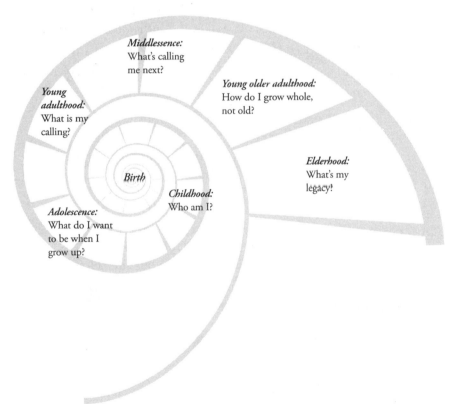

Middlessence:
What's calling
me next?

Young older adulthood:
How do I grow whole,
not old?

*Young
adulthood:*
What is my
calling?

Elderhood:
What's my
legacy?

Birth

Childhood:
Who am I?

Adolescence:
What do I want
to be when I
grow up?

camps until they were liberated. Frankl attributed his own and others' survival to the power of having a sense of purpose that kept their focus on meaningful actions ahead.

Purpose can help us survive challenges as well, and more than just survive—actually thrive as we make a difference in the world.

Ernest Becker, in *The Denial of Death*, claims, "The fear of death is the basic fear that influences all others; a fear from which no one is immune no matter how disguised it may be."[7] Rollo May adds, "The confronting of death gives the most positive reality to life itself. It makes the individual existence real, absolute, and concrete. Death is the one fact of my life which is not relative but absolute and my awareness of this gives my existence and what I do each hour an absolute quality."

Purpose is immortal. To face death squarely is to face purpose squarely. Mysteriously, the creative spirit of the universe calls us at various times and in various ways to make our own difference in the work of the universe—to fulfill our own special design.

Look back over the phases of your own life spiral. What were your core questions during each phase of your life? How did you frame the core questions at each phase? What is your core question today?

Chapter 4

The Gift of Purpose

Service is not possible unless it is rooted in love and nonviolence. The best
way to find yourself is to lose yourself in the service of others.

Mahatma Gandhi

Life purpose is a gift that you give naturally and spontaneously.
Remember those times when people you care about wanted you
to share with them? Maybe they were in need and asked for your
contribution. Think about what you love doing and what you
want to contribute naturally. What do you want to give others
that would make a difference for them? What is it that you see
naturally, that you would like them to see for themselves?

Your life purpose is a gift for three reasons. First, you
didn't have to earn it—it came with
your birth. Second, it is a gift
because you get something
for yourself when you
interact on purpose.
And third, it is a gift
to others because
they get something
from you that is
theirs to keep.
This chapter
will help you real-
ize that you are
uniquely gifted for

35

serving others, and will show how your own story can help you uncover your purpose, gifts, and passions.

Think of Yourself in a New Way

If you want to uncover your life purpose, you must think of yourself in a new way. What gifts do you bring to serving others? Do you awaken, inspire, ignite, support? Can you persuade, challenge, teach, coach, direct? Are you naturally moved to create, design, organize, compose, master? Can you help, befriend, listen, love, accept, share? Do you seek, heal, liberate, enable, achieve?

Your life purpose is what is unique and powerful about you, the qualities you express naturally and spontaneously. Right now, without further work or education, you have a gift to give in the area of your life purpose. There is something that you do that comes from the inside of you that you actively want to give to others. This gift of life purpose is given to you to give away to others. Purpose is an active quality.

Don't think too much about the answer to the following four questions—your first response will be your best:

What do people consistently come to you for or ask you for?

What gift do you consistently give to others that they consider to be your natural asset?

What gift makes you feel really alive and vital when you give it?

What gift do you possess that could be of real service to others if you developed it?

Are You Suppressing Your Idealism?

Late one afternoon in September 1915, Albert Schweitzer was sitting on the deck of a small steamboat making its way up the Ogooue River to Lambarene in Central Africa. He was bringing medical services to the local population in French Equatorial Africa. The boat was moving cautiously through a herd of hippopotamuses in the river. As Schweitzer watched the ship's captain maneuver to avoid hitting the animals, he came to a profound realization—the captain represented the highest purpose: reverence for the life of other creatures. For years Schweitzer had been searching for the key purpose in the modern world. He found it in Africa—"reverence for life."

Schweitzer recognized an expression of idealism in the care that the ship's captain was taking to avoid injuring the animals. Yet Schweitzer also observed that far more people are idealistic than will admit to being so:

> Just as the rivers are much less numerous than
> underground streams, so the idealism that is visible
> is minor compared to what men and women carry in
> their hearts, unreleased or scarcely released. Mankind
> is waiting and longing for those who can accomplish
> the task of untying what is knotted and bringing the
> underground waters to the surface.[8]

It's an odd quirk that makes us suppress our idealism. Opportunities for aligning our lives with our ideals are virtually everywhere. Using our gifts to serve others, observed Schweitzer, leads to happiness: "The only ones among you who will be really happy are those who have sought and found how to serve."

Off to a Flying Start

Caroline Otis had been a writer by trade for more than twenty years. Her work had allowed her to use and develop important gifts, and its freedom had allowed her to work at home and schedule her days around the needs of her family. Over the years, many questioning friends asked her, "Why are you so happy all the time?" Caroline's answer was that "my life is a blend of work, mom-ness, community involvement, physical expression, and singing in the choir."

As her children left for college, it became clear that parenting had been her most purposeful work. This realization—that helping young people move toward the future with confidence and a sense of joy—moved Caroline to consider working with other adolescents to help them get off to a flying start.

Caroline's purpose became "helping young people to discover their purpose, to identify and develop their strengths and passions, and to tear into the world of work with energy and joy."

She grew up believing that if she couldn't be the best at something, why bother to try? When she hit midlife, however, it became clear to her that "anything worth doing is worth doing badly." She learned more from trying something new—no matter how bad at it she was—than doing what she was already good at.

So Caroline joined a gospel choir—not because she was good at singing but because she loved to sing, especially gospel music. The choir has been a great lesson, because gospel singing is about emptying yourself out so the spirit can flow into you and out of you. It isn't about performing well but about giving what you've got.

In that gospel spirit—and because she loves movies—she took a sabbatical after her children left home to work on the crew of *Lone Star*, the film by the writer, director, and editor John Sayles, who is also a novelist. She said, "I worked on the film as a cable puller in the sound department—and I was a pretty inept cable puller, at that!" But she learned a lot about filmmaking and about herself.

When Caroline attended the film's preview at the South by Southwest Film Festival, she was struck by a question from the audience. A man asked John Sayles if he ever got discouraged and thought about not being a writer and filmmaker anymore. And John replied that he doesn't think of himself as a writer. He doesn't define himself as a filmmaker. He just gets passionate about stories, he said, and he loves to find the best ways to tell those stories—whether by the written word or by film. For John, his purpose is anchored solidly in finding and telling the stories that move him.

For Caroline, the quantum leap became to find work that she loves and to give herself to it—"off to her own flying start!" Her purpose and passion is to help adolescents "get off to a flying start in life."

Through purpose, we are more responsive to ourselves, just as artists are more in touch with themselves when absorbed in the creation of a painting. There is a selflessness that goes with absorption in something we genuinely find interesting; yet it is also a sense of being more ourselves.

What Is Your Story?

Every one of us eventually faces our own story, the time when we are challenged to define our life on this planet, our reason for being here. Our story often surfaces when our standard answers to the big questions no longer satisfy us. Nothing shapes our lives as much as the questions we ask — or refuse to ask — throughout our lives.

On the first day of each new year, and about every ten years, my gaze turns inward toward fresh questions. Eventually, however, I seem to arrive back at the beginning with the age-old purpose questions — the toughest yet essential ones.

How do you answer the essential questions? The differences in the quality of our lives often lie in the quality of the questions that shape our stories. And without each of our stories, the story of the universe would be incomplete.

The question What is my story? interests many of us as we age. Many of my friends, colleagues, and clients, who several years ago would have been reluctant to discuss their stories, are now talking openly about spiritual journeys, meaningful work, and legacy relationships. My own answer to the question is still evolving and deepening after many years of shaping it. My life has been a history of uncovering and integrating more elements of my self into my life.

On my way to becoming a school psychologist, I became a life coach, an executive educator, an author, and an expedition leader. In my early twenties, I was a counseling psychology graduate student with the military draft board hounding me to complete my studies and begin my compulsory military service. In an effort to find a solution I could live with during a war I didn't support, I joined an army psychological operations reserve unit. That choice required me to leave my schooling in Colorado with my master of arts and return to Minnesota.

Along with the move came the necessity of supporting my family. During my job-hunting process, I accidentally discovered the corporate human resources field. Joining a large Fortune 100 company, I worked under a great mentor in a variety of human resource positions, ending up, after two years, as training manager. In my training role, I had the opportunity to coach a large number of employees who were unclear about their career direction.

I knew from my counseling psychology training that there were many effective ways of helping people clarify their focus and direction. In the late 1960s, however, there were few practical books or programs available. So, I started creating my own ideas, exercises, and programs and trying them out after hours. Soon I had a burgeoning career coaching practice after hours, a growing reputation, and a waiting list!

With a growing family and financial needs, I moved to a large bank holding company, where, in addition to a much larger human resources job, I continued to hone my career coaching skills both inside the organization and after hours. However, I was still a lone voice in the career wilderness.

A chance meeting with Richard Bolles fueled my career coaching fires and affirmed my evolving coaching philosophy. Dick gave me the opportunity to preview what was later to become his forty-year best-selling book, *What Color Is Your Parachute?* From Dick, a former Episcopalian priest, I received support for my intuitive feeling that every individual has been created with a mission in life. Dick helped me clarify a belief for which I am eternally grateful: "The gifts of each of us and the value of serving others provide our mission in life." Dick sparked my interest in studying about purpose—a passion that has guided my work and remains with me to this day.

A chance meeting with author Sigurd Olson also fed my passion about purpose. I wanted to write about purpose. As a budding writer, I had heroes and models I wanted to imitate, and Sigurd Olson was one of them.

Sigurd was a wilderness philosopher and ardent conservationist who wrote about nature and spirituality. He focused on the purpose moment that we feel when we're in the presence of nature. I was deeply moved by his writing, and his books found their way into both my backpack and my briefcase.

I corresponded with him over several years, and he encouraged my purpose and my writing. In an essay on his own writing in his book *Open Horizons,* he wrote: "Occasionally, when I did no writing at all, my spirits fell and everything seemed without meaning or purpose."[9] The cure, he advised, was to begin again. When he began writing again, his spirit soared. He said that he wrote about things as he saw them and the passion just came through. When I was down or blocked in my writing, Sigurd inspired me to begin again, to follow my passion.

During this same time period, I applied for and received a Bush Foundation Fellowship to study adult development and positive aging issues. I designed my own nondegree, customized fellowship (few programs were available at the time) in an informal arrangement with the Harvard Business School. Through my fellowship studies, I discovered the need for and value of purpose in older people's lives.

After my fellowship studies, I quickly moved into full-time career coaching work. I studied it intensely and seemed to have a natural gift for it. I launched a successful one-to-one coaching practice. From that start I moved to leading workshops, cowriting my first book, speaking to groups, and guiding wilderness renewal expeditions.

Helping others discover their purpose became my purpose. It chose me. I uncovered my purpose on the way to somewhere else. Today my purpose is "to help people uncover the power of purpose." It moves me. It gets me up in the morning, excited to go to work. And it fulfills my need to connect deeply with people's lives — to give my gifts.

As I have had the profound privilege to listen to thousands of people's stories over the last three decades, my point of view on purpose has deepened. This book represents my understanding of what I have learned about the paths to purpose. There are three essential paths to purpose. To uncover your purpose, you must:

- Uncover your core.
- Uncover your gifts.
- Uncover your passions.

Uncover Your Core

Through wise teachers and elders, I became aware that we are born with a purpose. We live in a purposeful universe. Every organism in the universe has a design — a pattern that determines its function and role. A critical part of our development is the inside-out search for that core pattern. The

true joy in life is to turn ourselves inside out to uncover that
our purpose already exists within.

Each life has a natural, built-in reason for being. That
reason is to make a positive contribution to the world around
it. Purpose is the creative positive spirit of life moving through
us, from the inside out. It is the deep, mysterious dimension
in each of us—our core essence—where we have a profound
intuitive sense of who we are, where we came from, where we
are going, and how we fit in the world.

Each of us has a quest built into our essence. Otherwise,
we would not, in our deepest moments, ask: Who am I? What
am I meant to do here? What is the meaning of my life? Our
life quest is shaped by the inside-out questions we ask, or fail
to ask, during purpose moments.

Uncover Your Gifts

Purpose feeds our three deep spiritual hungers: to connect
deeply with the power of choice in our lives; to actively know
that we have a unique voice in the world; and to use our gifts
to make a difference in the world.

Our voice is the gifts of spirit in us, but we must uncover the
gifts and choose the calling in which we express them. When
we work and live on purpose, we bring together the needs of the
world with our special gifts in a vocation, or calling.

Uncover Your Passions

Purpose is what moves us. It is the conscious choice of what,
where, and how to make a positive contribution to our world.

Oliver Wendell Holmes wrote, "Many people die with their music still in them."[10] Our "music" is a metaphor for the quality or passion around which we choose to center our lives. Once we uncover our music—what moves us—life takes on a new energy. Our music is so powerful that we find we can hardly refrain from moving to its rhythm. It compels us to "dance," to take action.

Our world is incomplete until each one of us discovers what moves us. No other person can hear our music calling. We must listen and act on it for ourselves. To hear it, we need a positive environment that supports deep listening and truth telling.

In the power of our questions lies the power of purpose. To hear our music, we need a regular practice of solitude to listen to our deepest yearnings. The purpose quest requires the wisdom of questioning and listening.

Use the following guideline to uncover purpose in your life: "My purpose in life is to uncover my music." Take a pencil and paper and write an initial draft purpose statement: "My music in life is _____." Then, in a sentence or two, try to state clearly how you want to use your gifts to make a difference in the world.

If determining your purpose seems beyond reach now, take a segment of it, a day, for example, and put that in writing: "My music moment for today is _____."

Take your time, but keep at it until you have a statement that moves you. We will continue to look at the essence of purpose—the three paths—in the next section.

Part II

Paths to Purpose

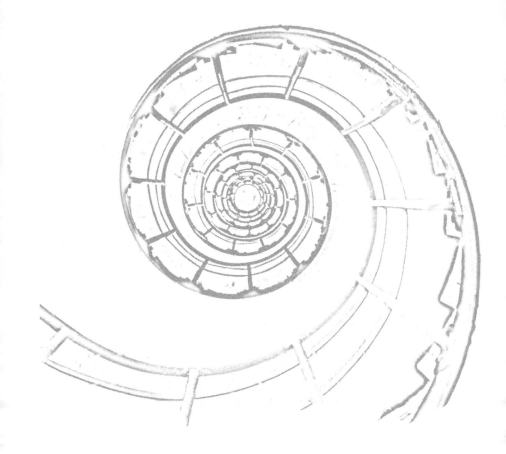

Chapter 5

Uncovering Your Purpose

We can discover this meaning in life in three different ways: (1) by doing a deed; (2) by experiencing a value; and (3) by suffering.

Viktor Frankl

Where do you start? How do you decide where to commit yourself? How do you uncover your purpose or calling? Many of us are starved for alignment in our lives. Purpose can serve as an aligning focus for our gifts, passions, and values. The most effective people know how to focus their daily activities while keeping their eye on a longer-range purpose, the ideals they want to align their lives around.

Purpose has a way of focusing time and energies around itself; that is the real power behind the purpose! It often involves refocusing our lives in order to bring out our voice and full music. This chapter will help you identify what moves you, show three ways to find your purpose, and challenge you to simplify your life to focus on your purpose.

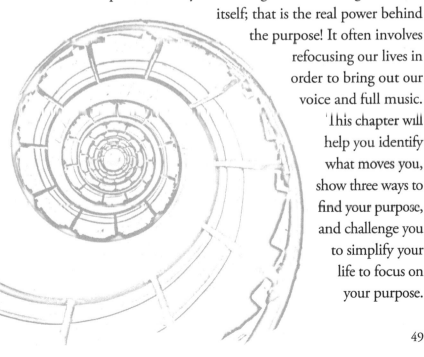

What Calls You?

Our life work is the purpose we live by transformed into action. If we open our eyes to the world around us, we often notice the endless "work" that calls for our energies and talents.

- Which parts or issues of the newspaper interest you?
- Which TV specials are you drawn to watch?
- Which parts of your organization's mission or strategy interest you?
- What speeches or presentations have moved you?
- Which "on-purpose" leaders inspire you?
- Which special-interest Web sites do you visit regularly?
- What needs of your mosque, church, synagogue, temple, or spiritual organization interest you?
- What part of your political party's platform moves you?

For most of us, the community in which we live is rich with possibilities for uncovering and expressing our purpose. To uncover our purpose, we need to detect—to sense—the potential issues that move us to action in the world.

Viktor Frankl points the way: "We can discover this meaning in life in three different ways: by doing a deed; by experiencing a value; and by suffering."

"Doing a Deed"

One way to start is to "uncover" what's needed and wanted, and then produce it—right where we are—in our current work, family, spiritual organization, or community.

Eric Utne speaks with the confidence of someone who has heard it all before. Yet at the same time, his words carry the caution of someone who has been carefully scrutinized by the media. Eric is the founder of both the *New Age Journal* and the *Utne Reader.* His purpose for the latter was to "help the world become a little greener and a little kinder."

That is still his mission today. But now he's on a quest to become a little greener and a little kinder himself. Eric's ability to see the big picture, his intense curiosity, and his commitment to social change often caused him to take himself a bit too seriously. He says his purpose now is to "find and follow my heart."

Eric took a sabbatical from the *Utne Reader* to embark on a journey to discover a more soulful approach to life. He felt pulled to spend more time at home with his family. He felt that the very character traits that helped build the magazine were now in the way of growing. During a twelve-day "vision fast" in the high desert of Death Valley, Eric slept and reflected alone for four days and four nights. He recalls, "There was a new stirring of energy within me. I realized that my life is now more about relationships and energy and less about work."

Eric left the magazine to serve two years as a classroom teacher, and he now organizes and promotes Community Earth Councils—groups of elders (people aged fifty plus) and young people (sixteen to twenty-eight years old) working together to address global environmental and social challenges at the local level. Community Earth Councils build community, helping young people find meaning and purpose while providing elders with a way to give back, inspire, and have an impact on the future. Through this effort, Eric has been able to focus energy and relationship building to make communities (and himself) greener and kinder.

John Horan-Kates felt a need is to promote "purposeful leadership" in his community of Vail, Colorado. He combined his passions for family, the mountains, and Christian education, together with his gifts as an idea developer, and founded the Vail Leadership Institute. As president, John brings together leaders to build the "purposeful valley" he wants to live in. The Vail Leadership Institute researches, designs, and delivers new programs to promote and facilitate purposeful living. John pours his gifts into his community to produce "what's needed," and in doing so he finds meaning.

Visible achievement and accomplishment of deeds—especially those we have had something to say about creating—are important. For deeds to have a real impact at a personal level, we must own the issue in a personally committed way. Claiming some deed set by others or expected of us is not nearly as satisfying. This, however, does not mean that whatever deed we select needs to be visible to others. It is "do-gooders" who need to keep score of their virtues. "Keeping score" may actually reduce our sense of contentment, as we clearly see how our commitment is driven by external (or ego) influences.

"Experiencing a Value"

We find meaning when our behaviors reflect what we value, what is important to us, what character traits we treasure and want to express. If identified and clear to us, our values can guide us toward our purpose. The reverse is also true. When circumstances or our own weaknesses lead us to act counter to what we value, we feel poorly about ourselves.

Purpose calls us to be the unique individuals that we are. Tucked away just outside the town of Osceola, Wisconsin, is a place every person should know about. The Aveda Spa is synonymous with living from the inside out. Nasreen Koaser, who moved from her native India to work at the spa as an "image stylist," embodied its mission: "to promote and support continuous learning as a foundation for success and well-being." Today, as a self-employed hair stylist, Nasreen brings such love and healing touch to her work that people come from long distances to fill up her calendar months and even a year in advance. In our busy, fast-paced, overscheduled world, Nasreen awaits her clients with hot herbal tea, a kind word, a healing touch, and an open heart.

She strives to make people happy by helping them feel good about themselves. She says, "I love my work because I love my clients. Every day God gives me the opportunity to bring out the pure essence in my clients. That is my purpose and I am grateful for work that allows me to use my gifts in this way."

Rollie Larson, an eighty-eight-year-old retired psychologist, experiences the value of "listening" every day. He lives as a whole person, integrated in mind, body, and spirit, with the natural curiosity and enthusiasm for life of a much younger person.

Rollie states, "Purpose, for me, boils down to relationships. What goes on with me and other people, that's what gives joy to me. I tried seventeen different jobs before I found that my calling was working with people! Working with other people

— sharing, caring, listening, loving — gives me a spiritual connection. Part of my prayers each night are that I can make a difference in someone's life tomorrow."

Rollie's long, esteemed counseling career took him down many paths, including founding a school counseling department, training corporate executives, opening a private practice with his wife, Doris, and writing several books. What distinguishes Rollie is his special gift—a genuine capacity to listen deeply to others. His credo, "Listen to someone today," is well known to the hundreds of people he has touched over the years. He counsels people, "If you have to go through seventeen jobs to find your calling—do it! Start opening some other windows in your areas of interest. Ultimately, your work must be a turn-on; it must feel passionate."

Rollie has blended the spirit and curiosity of the child with the maturity and wisdom of age. He has uncovered his purpose.

Andrew Greeley, quoted in Phillip Berman's book *The Courage of Conviction,* said:

> It seems to me that in the last analysis there are only
> two choices: Macbeth's contention that life is a tale
> told by an idiot, full of sound and fury and signifying
> nothing, and Pierre Teilhard's "something is afoot in the
> universe, something that looks like gestation and birth."
> Either there is a plan and purpose—and that plan and
> purpose can best be expressed by the words "life" and
> "love"—or we live in a cruel, arbitrary, and deceptive
> cosmos in which our lives are a brief transition between
> two oblivions.[11]

Purpose is the value we want to center our lives around—the way we orient ourselves toward life. It is the way we make sense or meaning out of our lives. People like Nasreen Koaser and Rollie Larson choose to center their lives around the assumption that "something is afoot in the universe, something that looks like gestation and birth."

Daring to be ourselves—living our values—is a personal and difficult issue because it involves courage, which is uncomfortable for many people. And it is not something another person can do for us.

What values do you treasure and want to express in your daily life? How can you experience that value?

"Suffering"

There are crises that significantly reduce the quality of life for most of us. These situations are so devastating that our entire sense of meaning may slip, leaving us shaken or enraged. At such times, feelings of shock and of being in limbo are not uncommon. When we cope effectively, a purpose may actually be found or strengthened or made clearer. We often learn much about who we really are under conditions of "suffering." The following are examples of triggering events that cause us to reassess our purpose: the death of a loved one, divorce, marital separation, major illness or disability, loss of work, a major geographic move, retirement, a major financial gain or loss.

These kinds of events cause most of us, at least temporarily, to ask the large questions. Because our life spiral and basic sense of self are disrupted, we are reawakened to the purpose and meaning we need so much.

By letting go and trying something new, we can begin to consider the possibility of new roles and purpose. In the early phases, the process is one of a painful search for new external sources of pleasure to fill the void produced by loss. But with time, the uncertainties subside and gradually give way to hope about the future—a new vision of ourselves. Our priorities shift to growing in new ways. As we adapt to the change and normalize our lives, we feel empowered with new confidence and competence. And we feel the deep joy of living on purpose.

How have you grown through a loss you suffered? What new pathway opened? What new priority emerged?

Simplifying Our Lives for a Purpose

When we are moved by something, many things previously felt to be important fade in significance. If our purpose is authentic enough, it involves us deeply and aligns all areas of our life. We begin to eliminate what is irrelevant and just so much clutter. A simplification takes place, and we achieve clarity about ourselves and our lives. We don't need to pretend to be what we're not. We recognize what is of true importance. In his seminal book *Voluntary Simplicity,* Duane Elgin quoted these remarks from Richard Gregg, who coined the term *voluntary simplicity:*

> Voluntary simplicity involves both inner and outer
> condition. It means singleness of purpose, sincerity and
> honesty within, as well as avoidance of exterior clutter, of
> many possessions irrelevant to the chief purpose of life.

It means an ordering and guiding of our energy and our desires, a partial restraint in some directions in order to secure greater abundance of life in other directions. It involves a deliberate organization of life for a purpose.[12]

The way to spend our precious time and energy wisely is to know the purpose for which we live and then to deliberately simplify our lives accordingly.

Richard Peterson had been moving toward simplicity for many years. As the former president of Vail Associates and later of Durango Ski Corporation, Richard's mission was to bring joy to others. And, in the process, Richard has been rediscovering the joy in his own life. Today, he lives a simple yet varied life, with a life/financial coaching practice and membership on the boards of directors of several nonprofits.

During his executive tenure, he rarely had time for listening to a deeper call; his life was filled with doing, not listening. When he left the executive ranks, it still did not solve his "doingness" problem. He says, "My biggest challenge was simplifying and being fully present for life. Discovering my calling was not something that jumped out at me."

Richard relates, "The natural world is my spiritual teacher. It started when I started backpacking in the form of a connection with something bigger than me. I observed, through nature, that we're all connected in one big web. The web includes all life, like dogs, gardens, and people."

Richard's purpose today is "to nurture my own and others' spiritual growth; to demonstrate love and gratitude for all that I am by doing something every day that expresses love to a fellow human, animal, or plant; and to balance interaction with nature with helping others develop a healthy relationship with money and prosperity."

Richard found his purpose by simplifying his life. So where can you start to simplify? What can you let go of in order to have time to live and work on purpose?

Chapter 6

Uncovering Your Gifts

Many people die with their music still in them.

Oliver Wendell Holmes

The power in purpose means uncovering our gifts—those of which we're already aware and are motivated to master and those that are emerging that we would like to try or explore.

We each possess gifts and natural talents. This fundamental assumption has proved true for everyone whom I have coached over the past thirty years. Everyone is gifted in some way. Many of us might deny that this is the case simply because we have focused on our weaknesses rather than our strengths.

Although talents are a part of everyday vocabulary, few people try to state clearly what their natural gifts are. The power behind our purpose is knowing and using our most-enjoyed gifts. This chapter will help you answer these questions: What are my gifts? How can I best give my gifts to something in which I believe—a value, product, person, service, ideal, problem, or organization?

Everyone Is Gifted

We all have natural abilities and inclinations and find that certain things come easily to us. We may perform a talent so effortlessly that we forget we have it. This is a gift. We might not have had to pay the price to invest in this gift because it came so easily; we might have been born with it! We may never even have had to practice it extensively.

The Puritan ethic has convinced many of us that anything requiring hard work is valuable, and anything that comes easily and does not require hard work is worthless. About our gifts we often think, "This comes easily, so it must be easy for everyone." We underestimate its worth. Actually, our gifts are our most powerful talents of all. And to be fulfilled in our lives, we must uncover and express them.

Some researchers say that we have numerous talents and ways of experiencing our innate intelligence. The theory of multiple intelligences was first proposed by Howard Gardner, a Harvard University educator, in 1983. In his book *Frames of Mind,* he reported on his original studies, which concluded that all people have at least seven intelligences. He recently added an eighth.[13] These categories are summarized below. As you read, consider how you see yourself fitting into these eight areas. Which areas represent your most-enjoyed gifts?

1. **Verbal-linguistic: to think in words; to use language to express and understand complex meanings.** Do you like word games, puns, rhymes, or tongue twisters? Do you use

words correctly and persuasively? If you are attracted to this area, then tasks that require language—reading, writing, and speaking—are your natural talents. You are able to write clearly and can instruct or communicate through the spoken word. Sample work you might enjoy and excel in: attorney, journalist, poet, public relations director.

2. **Logical-mathematical: to connect cause and effect; to understand relationships among actions, objects, or ideas.** Do you use numbers effectively? Do you like facts, figures, or balancing your checkbook? If you are attracted to this area, then numbers and logic—reasoning, critical thinking, and mathematical problem solving—are your natural talents. You are able to make sense of your world by taking a rational, logical approach. Sample work for you: accountant, scientist, computer programmer, electrical engineer.

3. **Visual-spatial: to think in pictures; to perceive the visual world accurately.** Do you think visually? Do you have a vivid imagination or perceive colors, textures, shapes, and relationships among shapes accurately? If you are attracted to this area, then thinking in images and using shapes and colors to portray the world around you are your natural talents. You are able to visualize, draw, paint, or sketch your ideas and are easily oriented to three-dimensional spaces. Sample work: architect, pilot, artist, interior designer.

4. **Musical: to think in sounds, rhythms, melodies, and rhymes.** Do you like humming tunes, making them up, or singing along with the radio? Do you appreciate and understand musical composition? If you are attracted to this area, then rhythms and melodies—singing in tune,

keeping time to rhythms, and having an ear for music—are
your natural abilities. You are able to listen to and discern
different selections of musical pieces and appreciate
compositions of all kinds. Sample work: music teacher, choir
director, songwriter, musician, vocalist.

5. **Kinesthetic: to use the body in skilled and complicated ways
   for expressive activities.** Do you like to exercise, play sports,
   dance, or work with your hands? Do you move your body
   effectively and gracefully? If you are attracted to this area,
   then manipulating objects, demonstrating athletic prowess,
   and hands-on problem solving are your natural abilities. You
   are able to assemble things, build models, sculpt, dance, and
   enjoy physical activities of all kinds. Sample work: actor,
   dancer, athlete, choreographer, outdoor guide.

6. **Interpersonal: to think about and understand another
   person.** Are you sensitive to the feelings of others? Do
   you form successful relationships with others and enjoy
   teamwork? If you are attracted to this area, then tuning into
   the needs, feelings and desires of others—understanding
   and working with others—are your natural abilities. You
   are able to see the world from another's perspective and
   connect effectively with people in the world around you.
   Sample work: nurse, teacher, counselor, coach, physician,
   entrepreneur.

7. **Intrapersonal: to think about and understand oneself.**
   Do you like to meditate or ponder the imponderables? Do
   you enjoy solitude and reflection? If you are attracted to
   this area, then being self-reflective—aware of your deep
   self, your inner feelings and motivations—are your natural

abilities. You are able to spend time alone to reflect on the world around you in an independent, self-disciplined, and self-motivated way. Sample work: clergy, psychologist, executive/leader, philosopher, artist.

8. **Naturalistic: to understand the natural world, including plants, animals, and scientific studies.** Do you like to classify and analyze how things fit together? If you are attracted to this area, then sensing, understanding, and systematically classifying the natural world — the environment — are your natural abilities. You have an intuitive sense of how things fit together and are able to distinguish interrelationships in the world. Sample work: biologist, farmer, veterinarian, meteorologist.

Looking at gifts with Gardner's framework expands the possibilities for discovering our gifts. This framework enables us to place value on a broader range of abilities and helps us see our differences as strengths, as talents.

Early in life, we learn to feel that some talents are more valuable to society than others are. Thus, we often don't acknowledge our gifts because we say, How could I make a living doing that? or What economic value could that gift possibly have? Uncovering our gifts means overcoming the tendency to discredit our gifts as less worthy than others. Instead, we accept that we each have important gifts to share with the world.

Uncovering our gifts also means overcoming any arrogance that exaggerates our own gifts at the expense of the gifts of others. We can present our gifts without self-display; we don't need to pretend to be what we are not. There is nothing for others to see through. There is no significant gap between how we act and what we really feel. Our gifts are transparent, and our purpose has power.

If you're confused about what your gifts are, you can ask your spouse, a friend, a colleague, a supervisor, or someone who knows you very well to help you clarify and focus on your strengths. If you wish to spend the time and energy to uncover or confirm your talents in depth, you might consider doing the Calling Cards Exercise offered by The Inventure Group.[14]

Are You Bringing Your Gifts to Work?

The idea that we should find joy in our work is one that many people feel ambivalent about, both accepting and questioning. Yet it seems to make sense that we do best what we enjoy most, and when we use our gifts, we enjoy what we do.

Many years ago a close friend, Rolf, asked me, "Are you enjoying your work?" He had been reading the *Tao Te Ching*, which states, "In work, do what you enjoy." Actually, I had been asking myself that same question—but conveniently either not listening or denying my own response.

In answering my friend, I said, "Things are okay. I believe what I'm doing is making a contribution—you know—doing something worthwhile. But no, I don't feel like I'm really enjoying my work. In fact, I feel as though I'm waiting for something to happen—something to move me one way or another!"

The speed of my response surprised me. Actually, I had never considered work as joy. Work was work. I began reflecting on my friend's question. It gradually became clear to me that even if I was doing a worthwhile thing, if I was not enjoying it, something was wrong. Perhaps it was not the best use of my gifts.

Prompted by a purpose moment with a friend and confirmed through deeper reflection, I chose to make a radical change in my work life that made better use of my most enjoyed gifts, and in doing so found new joy in my work.

There's a pervasive idea that work is something to be tolerated and leisure is something to be enjoyed. Yet work consumes the most significant number of our waking hours. When we consider that we spend about 60 percent of our life's time working, common sense suggests that we discover and use our most enjoyed gifts. We can refuse to go to our graves with our music still inside us.

Drew Stirrat wanted more than anything else to travel and explore new lands. So, recalling the advice his father gave him — "If you're not doing what you love to do, now, you may never experience what you really want to do" — he hit the road.

He hiked the Pacific Crest Trail, drove the length of Africa, lived on a kibbutz in Israel, trekked through Asia, kayaked in the Arctic, and biked and backpacked throughout the United States. Between adventures, he worked as a contractor/laborer to build his bank account for the next escape.

After following his bliss for fifteen years, Drew decided it was time to settle into an appropriate career using the learnings from his travels. He became a program director for Outward Bound and found that many adults were coming to programs seeking the same sense of adventure that he had been pursuing much of his life.

Drew began using nature and adventure as metaphors for life's learning experiences, to help people rediscover themselves. Today, he creates environments where people can take risks. As a facilitator and life coach, he inspires and helps people find purpose and meaning in their lives. Drew's purpose is "to help people grow and rediscover their essence." Through his own gifts of listening, empowering, motivating, and coaching people to feel better about themselves, he helps people find more vitality in their work. And by doing what he enjoys, Drew finds vitality and meaning.

Our work takes up the largest chunk of our waking hours each week. To a large degree, it determines our quality of life, depending on the location of the work and the amount of money earned. Where we live, who we become friends with, and what opportunities come our way are influenced by the work we do.

When our work is not aligned with what we need and enjoy in basic ways, problems in performance can result, and advancement may be less likely. The mental and physical costs of personal frustration and stress can be high.

Thus, knowing ourselves—what we do well and enjoy doing—is important not only for making work and volunteer choices but also for empowering our purpose and living more satisfying lives. As you think about your present work or volunteer activities, ask yourself, Is this a good match for my most enjoyed gifts? As you consider new work or volunteer activities, ask, Is this likely to be a good match for my most enjoyed gifts?

Chapter 7

Uncovering Your Passions

This is the true joy in life, the being used for a purpose recognized by yourself as a mighty one; the being thoroughly worn out before you are thrown on the scrap heap; the being a force of Nature instead of a feverish selfish little clod of ailments and grievances complaining that the world will not devote itself to making you happy.

George Bernard Shaw

Now that you have considered your gifts—the power—where do you express them? For the sake of what? An important next step is to uncover what moves you. This is the hard part for many of us because we believe the old adage, "Anything worth doing is worth doing well." Most of the emphasis—mistakenly, I believe—has been put on the "worth doing well." The real question is "What is worth doing?"—a much-neglected question for many of us. What issues, interests, causes, or challenges capture your genuine enthusiasm? What keeps you up at night? What gets you up in the morning?

In the answers to questions like these, we can uncover our passions. Our passions, simply stated, are our obsessions—those things we care most deeply about. Whatever form they take, passions are identified by their vitality—they are "alive"; we feel them deeply. A passion moves us to action in the world. Moreover, a passion doesn't quit but keeps recurring in our thinking and experiences.

When you have a good idea of what your gifts are and what moves you, you will have two of the three key ingredients of the power of purpose (the third is your calling, discussed in Chapter 8). Life and work choices based on gifts and passion produce focus and energy. The answer to the question What's worth doing? will be different for each of us. This chapter will help you answer the question for yourself to help uncover your passions.

"Someone Oughta Do Something!"

When I wrote the first edition of this book, I worked at a small antique desk in my hundred-year-old, hand-hewn, immigrant log cabin in the north woods of Wisconsin. I was surrounded by books on the topic, so absorbed in my task I sometimes felt I was in an altered state of consciousness. I often lost track of time as idea after idea popped into my mind from some deep well of sources. According to Mihalyi Csikszentmihalyi, Distinguished Professor of Psychology at Claremont Graduate University, I was in "flow"—so passionate about my topic that I lost touch with time.

In his book *Flow: The Psychology of Optimal Experience*, Csikszentmihalyi states his belief that we come closest to total fulfillment when in the flow state. He has concluded from his research that a passionate drive to solve problems and meet challenges causes us to derive pleasure from performing at our peak. By finding ourselves in our passions, we lose ourselves in time.

To consider potential opportunities where we can plug in our gifts, we must "tap into the flow state"[15] to think of what needs move us in our work, our organization, our family, our community, or society in general, and then examine those problems, issues, or concerns that we feel passionate about. What are the needs of your family, neighborhood, community, business, spiritual organization, the world? What needs doing? What issues do you truly feel "someone oughta do something about"?

To stimulate your thinking, ask yourself these questions:

- If you were asked to create a TV special about something that moves you, what would it be about?

- What magazines intrigue you most at a newsstand? What sections or articles capture your attention?

- If you started a business or organization in order to solve a need, what would it be?

- What issue would you like to see someone write a best-selling book about?

- What subjects would you like to learn about? Go back to school for? Study under a master in?

- In the past year, what cause did you contribute to? What interests does it reflect?

- Who are the people you find yourself voluntarily getting

together with, again and again, for deeper discussions?
What are your deepest conversations obsessing about?

- How would you use a gift of a million dollars if it had to
be given away or designated for a cause, issue, or problem
that moves you?

- Is there any need or problem you believe in so strongly
you'd love to work at it full time if you were paid well to
do it?

There is an old East African Swahili saying: *kuisi kwingi,
koura mengi.* Roughly translated, it means that when you
live a long life, you see and learn a lot. For me, the truth of
this saying is powerful and profound. During the writing of
this new edition, I spent time thinking about this saying and
what I have learned since I wrote the first edition. One key
learning is about the healthy power of curiosity. No matter
where we are in the lifespan, we need to consistently uncover
our curiosity.

The Power of Curiosity

I just turned sixty-five. My Medicare card just arrived, triggering
a new curiosity about positive aging. Today, we "seasoned citizens," who represent one of the largest demographic segments
in the United States, have a serious curiosity for learning.

My own curiosity about aging began when I was in fifth
grade. My church youth group volunteered at a local nursing
home to cheer up the folks by reading and singing. The odors,
the wheelchairs—coupled with the piercing moans and yells
of a few residents—stayed with me for a long time. In fact,

it wasn't until I reached age twenty-nine and received a Bush Foundation Fellowship to study positive aging that my perspective on aging shifted.

And now, at age sixty-five, it is shifting again. I have seen and learned a lot, and I love being this age and working with people this age who have curiosity. Nothing is worse, for me, than being stuck on an airplane or at a dinner party next to a "former" anything—former executive, former teacher, former scientist. My strong preference is to sit next to someone who has a powerful curiosity about just about anything!

Walking the Great Wall in China, looking at the moon through a powerful telescope, saving a wild and scenic ruin, building a home with Habitat for Humanity, becoming a mentor for Big Brothers/Big Sisters. What do these have in common? They all are evidence of deep curiosity.

In my day-to-day life, I encounter people who seem driven by something outside themselves, whose passion for their work or volunteer activities, their community, or their cause seems to rise above the possible. Indeed, we say that in such people we see the power of purpose. I sense that their lives are guided by a powerful curiosity—something more important than simple survival, something not merely intellectual, either—something in their souls.

It's beyond our power as human beings to look into the souls of our fellow human beings to measure their power of hope or curiosity. Our best possibility for understanding, let alone replicating, this inner fire that contributes so greatly to the world is to study their present passions, their stories, the look in their eyes when they are working, the joy they bring to those around them.

"What Are You Good At? How Can You Help?"

Neil Lovell and Jane Caldwell are two such people whom I met in London. Both work for the nonprofit charity, Kids Company. Kids Company was founded by Camila Batmanghelidjh to provide practical, emotional and educational support to vulnerable children and young people from the most deprived areas of London. Camila's deep passion to create a best-practice model of care to be replicated nationwide prompted Neil and Jane to take a major leap and join the Kids Company movement. I never met Camila, but her purpose was a palpable presence in the room.

Before joining Kids Company, Jane had established three companies in which she was the creative director. She also had worked as an independent film producer making documentaries and feature films, including the multiple-award-winning film *Foreign Moon,* directed by Zhang Zeming. She produced music promos for Sony and has written and directed plays for the theater. So why would she leave all this behind to join Kids Company? Jane sums it up in one word: "passion." She now directs the hugely successful arts program, encompassing visual arts, fashion, music, drama, and dance.

"The majority of those kids who seek our help suffer from severe emotional and behavioral difficulties resulting from significant experiences of trauma and neglect," Jane explains. "Many are 'lone children' living in chronic deprivation, with limited or no support from the adults in their life. I can relate to this in my own life experience."

Neil came to Kids Company with more than twenty-two years of broad communications, marketing, and business experience in agencies and in-house roles for big organizations. "Most of the organizations I have worked in have undergone significant change, including rebranding and mergers and acquisitions communications," relates Neil. "Over time," he says, "it wore me down. I needed to rekindle the flame."

Now Neil directs fund-raising and external relations at Kids Company, and he sums up his new feeling toward work as "passion." He says, "Kids Company's aim is to promote and support emotional well-being. Our approach is rooted in 'attachment theory,' which I am deeply curious about. We are pioneering in the areas of child abuse, neglect, and trauma, and have received support and recognition from the government to replicate our work in other areas."

Neil and Jane both experienced purpose moments upon meeting Camila. She asks only two questions: "What are you good at?" and "How can you help?" In answering these questions, Neil said, "My story suddenly made sense, what I was here to do. Finally I could see how it all fit together—how my life up to this point had, in fact, prepared me to meet Camila." Jane realized, "A lot of money didn't really do it for me. I yearned for a cause, a passion to guide my work. Camila modeled that and I wanted it, too."

Jane and Neil, along with others, are helping to lead Kids Company to the next level of effectiveness by bringing their gifts and passions, plus experiences from their past work lives, to create the future for Kids Company. In doing so, they are also creating a more meaningful future for themselves.

With age and life experience can come a feeling of freedom and liberation to pursue our passions. We are now, hopefully, more mature. We have gained practical wisdom about what's worth doing with our time, talents, and money. Our value systems have shifted away from self-absorption toward generativity—giving back to life. For people like Jane and Neil, passion is a powerful thing. They were willing to take big risks on things they care about.

Bringing Life and Livelihood Together

Theologian Matthew Fox writes, "A spirituality of work is about bringing life and livelihood back together again. And spirit with them." He claims, "Spirit means life, and both life and livelihood are about living in depth, living with meaning, purpose, joy, and a sense of contributing to the greater community."[16]

Sally Humphries Leider, my spouse and purpose partner, said, "I always felt natural doing what I was doing. I love to teach children, to bring out their essence, their spirit." Throughout her life, Sally has immediately connected with children as her natural learning partners. Ever since she was in the third grade, Sally was in awe of teachers. She says, "My fantasy was to be able to sit on the ground outdoors with my second-grade teacher and just talk."

When Sally started her teaching career in the city, she missed the out-of-doors most of all. Having grown up on a river in natural surroundings, she says, "I was given the gift of place—the gift of growing up in a place which was rich with the sounds, sights, and smells of nature. I took place for granted until my parents died and I couldn't go back to the river anymore." She tried to find the same feeling in other places but couldn't find it. So, she moved back to the river—a place she loves and is passionate to preserve.

Sally's parents were active in support of the environment, willing to fight, lobby, and educate people about preserving the natural river valley they lived in. Sally carries on their battle. Today, as a professional environmental educator, activist, and life coach, Sally says her purpose is "to instill the love of the natural world in people of all ages." She feels a legacy to continue the hard work her parents left her of maintaining the natural harmony in nature. Through her Watershed Wisdom classes at the local schools, and her Wild Indigo coaching practice with young women in transition, she inspires people to develop a deep sense of place. Her parents gave her the place, growing up, to love nature and notice things in nature. They taught her what's worth saving and preserving and working for.

Sally's deep passion is biodiversity—harmony with nature, not dominance over nature. She believes in the intrinsic value of all nature, rather than the idea that the natural environment is a resource for human exploitation. She believes that "biodiversity, the total variety of life on earth, is collapsing at mind-boggling rates. The accelerating loss of plant and animal species is occurring all over the planet."

To stop the losses, Sally believes that a critical aspect of awareness for all of us is to experience nature directly. She says, "To the extent that we can discover for ourselves a special connection with the natural world, we will be potentially motivated to take action to preserve the earth's species and ecosystems. That's my purpose, to give people that experience."

At the end of *Flow*, Csikszentmihalyi offers a prescription for the power of purpose. He says we can transform our whole life into a unified flow experience by approaching our activities in a certain way, by pursuing what he calls a "life theme."

Whatever our passion, "as long as it provides clear objectives, clear rules for action, and a way to concentrate and become involved, any goal can serve to give meaning to a person's life."

Can you detect a life theme in your activities? Are you pursuing it?

Part III

Working on Purpose

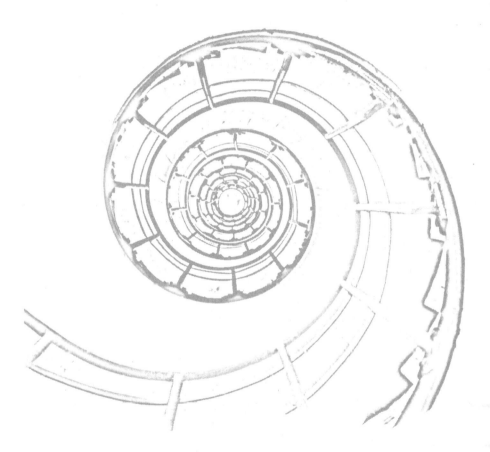

Chapter 8

How Do I Heed the Call?

This book is about a search, too, for daily meaning as well as daily bread, for recognition as well as cash, for astonishment rather than torpor; in short, for a sort of life rather than a Monday through Friday sort of dying.
Studs Terkel

Earlier in human history, people offered their daily activities as a thank you to God, because all enterprise was ultimately intended for God. This was the basis for the infamous work ethic, with which many people have an ambivalent relationship. However, the concept of stewardship, by which one made an offering to God of one's best efforts, elevated a person's work to the status of a calling.

A calling comes from the inside out; it is the expression of our essence, our core. Our calling is an expression of the spirit at work in the world through us. It is that mysterious voice that calls us to find our voice and to play our music. A calling means bringing spirit to work. A calling calls forth the deeper questions of work, such as how, why, and for whom we do our work.

Once you have some understanding of your gifts and have identified your passion, the third key ingredient that powers your purpose is your calling. A calling adds the concept of service to passion and gifts. Every individual is by creation essentially a servant. And this is possible because each of us has been born with certain unique gifts. We are accountable to God for how they are used, misused, or not used at all.

So now we face the question: Is work a job—a way to pay the bills, something to be endured—or can work be synonymous with a calling? This chapter will help you explore the idea of calling and what it takes to heed your call.

Calling and Motivation

My coaching work involves helping people become clearer about the presence or absence of a calling in their work. Since I became passionate about the importance and benefits of the call in work, I have made a practice of interviewing people I meet who seem "called to" their work. This helps to test my hypothesis that high motivation is associated with a connection to some higher purpose or calling.

Of course, many people who report to work every day are cynical and burned-out—they have given up and seem content to make it to quitting time. Many people genuinely feel overworked. In the words of the German mystic Meister Eckhart, they are "worked" instead of working. Many believe it is ethically important for them to work hard, though they don't see any larger common good deriving from their work.

However, the people who perform most energetically, creatively, and enthusiastically are those who believe they are contributing to a mission, purpose, or cause outside of and larger than themselves. The failure of many organizations to enlist people in some kind of unselfish, nonquantitative mission is at the root of many productivity problems today. When we ignore purpose at work, we inhibit our highest motivator.

Finding and heeding a call—a work mission that goes beyond ourselves—has many naturally productive consequences. It provides us with a source of deep energy. We are clear about how others may benefit from our efforts. A call provides guidance for our conduct and a focus for spending our precious time meaningfully.

The notion of heeding the call may take a while to digest. It requires an openness of the heart and—above all—patience. The discovery of our calling often requires an incubation period. The architect Le Corbusier said that the birth of a project was just like the birth of a child: "There's a long period of gestation ... a lot of work in the subconscious before I make the first sketch. That lasts for months. One fine morning the project has taken form without my knowing it." The "birth" of one's calling may feel like this.

Most of us want to feel that we are significant and that our work calls us to something enduring and worthwhile. More than anything else, naturally productive work enables us to spend our precious time in ways consistent with our gifts, passions, and values.

The Call

Sometimes a call can come literally, if we have ears and heart to hear. Craig Neal, a self-described mystic-organizer, states, "I remember the day I first thought about my purpose, during the 1963 March on Washington. There I was, standing right in front of the Lincoln Memorial during Martin Luther King, Jr.'s 'I have a dream' speech. That speech shifted my life, forever. I went from an oblivious sixteen-year-old suburban New Jersey high school kid to a spiritual seeker."

During Craig's ensuing career, he sought to work only for organizations and people who had strong values. He eventually joined Garden Way, an organization dedicated to saving the world through gardening, and he also worked on founding the *Harrowsmith* and *Organic Gardening* publications.

He came to a purpose moment during his five-year stint as publisher of the *Utne Reader* that business is the most powerful force for change on the planet. "What hit me," Craig recalled, "is that everyone works and that the purpose of work was to provide a service. I was happiest when I was serving others or working in companies whose service aided the natural evolution of the planet."

Craig's call was to start organizing around the "big questions." So he got involved with emerging organizations such as Business for Social Responsibility and Social Venture Network. He began to see more clearly how many people didn't know how to "serve and make a living." He saw how they compromised for so much less than they knew they could give to their work.

To help people share their personal gifts with their organizations and to help organizations nurture and give back to their workers, Craig cofounded the Heartland Circle. Its mission is "to integrate personal growth and social transformation by cultivating healthier individuals, families, workplaces, and communities." Heartland helps achieve this through the development of local and national "thought leader gatherings" and related consulting and publishing ventures.

The Heartland Circle also supports courageous conversation in the workplace. Through learning events like Thought Leader Gatherings and the Art of Convening Trainings, Craig is helping to steer the Heartland Circle toward an important role in the twenty-first century. He is driving himself and others to find both daily bread and daily meaning.

Craig reflects on his journey: "What it all boils down to is courage. It's not mystical; it's practical. If the human spirit already, as I believe, embodies everything, the question is one of courage. What am I willing to do, at this moment?"

All Are Called — Few Choose

I meet many people today who are letting go of their work to find new work. They feel called.

The lives of people who have an obvious calling or purpose in life are fascinating. They are read about, talked about, and sometimes used as models for living a life that matters. Their lives invite questions of why they were chosen and how they recognized their calling.

A deeper call consciously started for Dan Petersen when he completed his studies to become an orthodontist. Looking back, Dan says, "I was operating with an undeclared purpose

to set my life up with enough money and enough time to follow my longing for adventure. I wanted to work half of the
year and be adventurous with the other half."

And Dan did just that for twenty-two years. At that point,
he left a successful private practice to follow his calling to
study holistic healing. He recalls, "Something very powerful
was calling me; so powerful, I was willing to give up almost
everything to discover it. It was in the form of a question:
How does self-healing occur?"

He left his practice to return to school to study his
passion—the body-mind connection. He believed that self-
healing systems function optimally when we remove the
habits and hindrances to normal growth.

Dan's purpose today is "to create the conditions for
change." He has the same calling he had fifteen years ago
but in a new form. As a personal transformation coach, he
provides an environment in which the body, mind, emotions,
and spirit can self-heal by creating conditions for a deeper
understanding of oneself and the world we live in.

Dan believes that the optimal environment for human life
is "freedom of expression, meaningful purpose, compassion,
and balance." His purpose continues to evolve and broaden to
encompass "creating the conditions for the transformation of
human consciousness."

Dan's calling came by being open to his passions, being
aware of what was pulling on his heart, changing his course,
and courageously putting a plan into action.

The Call for Courage

We find the call from inside ourselves. We sense that there is something unique and special that we can contribute and that the kind of life, work, or volunteer work we do should align with these contributions. Heeding the call starts when our "music"—an aim, a passion, an interest, a problem, an idea—attracts us enough to move us to action on its behalf. It is important enough so that focusing on it directs our activities and gives our lives meaning.

We all have had many opportunities—purpose moments—that could lead us to heed the call in our lives. The question we must ask ourselves is Was I present when the opportunity presented itself? Heeding the call requires that we be present in our life, making choices that are aligned with what we care most about. Heeding the call also requires courage.

Are you ready to take the next step toward making a difference? Can you recognize that there is a next step waiting for you to take? Can you find the courage to look for that step and follow where it leads?

Chapter 9

How Do I Work on Purpose?

The true test of a servant-leader is this: Do those around the servant-leader become wiser, freer, more autonomous, healthier, and better able themselves to become servants? Will the least privileged of society be benefited or at least not further deprived?

Robert Greenleaf

In my years as a life coach, I have seen many people who do not connect deeply with their work. Some people measure success in strictly financial terms. Others have a broader definition of success, but their vision is not consistent with the purpose of the organization for which they work. And judging by the dramatic rise in the number of stress-related problems among workers at all levels, many feel alienated from any meaning in their work.

This chapter will explore the meaning of success and provide a tool to help you determine if your work is on purpose.

What Is Success?

Toward what success do we strive? The work ethic, for many of us, does not seem to be dead or even dying. For some of us, success is the advancement of our careers. We will make tremendous sacrifices for a career, will bend over backward to avoid making waves to advance it, and will treat ourselves as resumés to be packaged and marketed to further it. The consequence of such an orientation to success is that we become motivated primarily by personal gain—what our work will get us.

Yet when we look beneath the surface of such a drive for success, what's there? The result is a person with highly refined skills of the head, but not of the heart—a person who knows how to work but not how to be happy or satisfied or relaxed.

In *The Overworked American,* economist Juliet Schor describes "the squirrel cage of work and spend" that traps so many people. "Happiness," she claims, "has failed to keep pace with economic growth."[17] There is a false belief that the next purchase will yield happiness, or if not that one, then the next. But that belief merely sets us up for the "squirrel-cage" mentality of "work, and spend, and work and spend some more." No matter how much we make, it is never enough. If we find no joy and meaning in the work we do, we will be stuck in this hopeless, unrewarding cycle.

However, there is another way. James Autry got it right when he wrote, "Work can provide the opportunity for spiritual and personal as well as financial growth. If it doesn't, we're wasting far too much of our lives on it."[18]

Modern society has given many of us the means to succeed financially and build apparently successful careers, but often we still cannot find true joy or a purpose to live for. We find that if we strive for success as an end in itself, we never find it. And we are tired of working for organizations that consume us and offer money in return for stressful and unfulfilling work.

Further, in a restructured, shifting economy, many people are being forced to reconsider the merits of conventional success—such as security, advancement, and retirement. These disenfranchised and discouraged workers are beginning to place a higher value on criteria that have deeper meaning, such as service, balance, community, and mission or purpose. They are asking: To what are we committed? Whom do we serve?

Finding Purpose at Work

Many people argue against the practicality of finding meaningful work. Rarely, however, does anyone argue against the idea or the desirability of such work.

The problem appears to be a gap between supply and demand of a most central thing—meaningful work—work that fully engages our talents in something we believe in. Perhaps one reason is that we don't really expect work to give us much meaning. I have observed at least four separate levels of work expectations:

- The first level is "it's just a job; any job is okay as long as the money is good and we can do our thing after work."
- The second level is that of a permanent job. At this level, "our work has to be regular; we need benefits, vacations, and . . . security."

- A third level is that of profession or trade. Rather than thinking only of money and security, "We want substance in our work. We want to grow our talents and be challenged." At this level, we are still profoundly concerned with money, but we are also attached to the profession, or work, itself.

- A fourth level is that of a calling. At this level, we realize that work is related to money but that work is also a path to use our gifts to make a difference doing something we believe needs doing in this world. We begin to consider the meaning that work can bring and the opportunity it allows us to follow a calling yet still have a marketable, income-producing involvement in the world.

The first step to finding work with purpose—or to find a purpose in your current work—is to determine what level you are now working on. The Working-on-Purpose Inventory can help.

The Working-on-Purpose Inventory

To find work that is a source of "daily meaning and daily bread" takes time and thoughtful analysis.

Take a few minutes to take the Working-on-Purpose Inventory in the Resources at the back of the book. What are the signs in your work that indicate, "Yes, my work is on purpose"? What are the signs that indicate "No, my work isn't as meaningful as I might wish"? Check either yes or no according to how you feel about each question today.

The total number of yes responses on the inventory provides a general idea of your power of purpose at work. If you have many yes responses, you're obviously fully aligned with your work. If you have many no responses, you probably lack a sense of purpose or direction, and you might consider further clarifying your gifts, passions, and values. The time taken to identify elements of purposeful work is well invested.

The True Test of a Servant-Leader

Many leaders are rediscovering the connection between purpose and serving. Warren Malkerson was vice president and general manager of a large sporting goods catalogue company. He had felt this connection through his whole life but didn't understand it until he was in a big job. As a senior leader, he relates, "I always got criticized for caring too much about people. I felt a struggle being on the 'soft side,' like the ugly duckling."

One day he realized he was, in fact, not the ugly duckling but a swan—that caring for people was not only worthwhile but also productive. Wherever he has worked, it has been said, "His people always seem to be the happier, more creative folks in the organization."

Warren believes there's a swan at the core of every one of us. His purpose is "to help others discover their swan—the core inside." He feels that every human is struggling to unlock his or her potential.

Warren views every job as a test of servant leadership. He considers his leadership to be effective when his employees say, "I've never worked so hard and learned so much. He makes me learn!" He pledges to people when he hires them that they'll always be able to answer yes to the question, "Was this one of your best learning experiences?"

Like one of his heroes, the late quality guru Edward Deming, Warren believes, "I don't have to convert everybody! I'm not a missionary. I'm not here to help those who don't want to be helped. But my purpose is to help those who want to learn on purpose!"

Leaders like Warren, who strive to serve their colleagues and organizations, who are committed to the growth of others, clearly see that the servant leadership way of doing business is productive and profitable, and at the same time it satisfies the desire people have to find personal meaning in their work.

A Servant-Leader in Action

Nelson Mandela's inaugural speech upon assuming the presidency of South Africa had a profound effect on Phil Styrlund's concept of servant leadership. Phil, a senior vice president of a large telecommunications company, was struck by a quote Mandela used from Marianne Williamson's book *A Return to Love:*

> Our deepest fear is not that we are inadequate. Our deepest fear is that we are powerful beyond measure. It is our light, not our darkness, that most frightens us. We ask ourselves, Who am I to be brilliant, gorgeous, talented, fabulous? Actually, who are you not to be? You are a child of God. Your playing small doesn't serve the world. There's nothing enlightened about shrinking so that other people won't feel insecure around you. We

are all meant to shine, as children do. We were born to make manifest the glory of God that is within us. It's not just in some of us; it's in everyone. And as we let our own light shine, we unconsciously give other people permission to do the same. As we're liberated from our own fear, our presence automatically liberates others.[19]

Phil had long believed that there is something large going on in the world—that we're living in a mystery larger than we as humans are able to comprehend. And he had a hunger, a calling, to play larger in that world.

In helping to lead his company, Phil had the privilege of being paid to do something that he liked, that he would do for free. He claims, "It's only through relationships that anything significant and sustainable can be achieved. As a leader, I find pleasure, beyond comprehension, being a small part of making other people's lives large. My purpose is to enlarge and dignify the lives of others." Phil has a personal calling to create an environment of servant leadership where people can speak their truth and express their gifts. He says, "Productivity is a natural outcome of using your gifts in a healthy environment."

Phil believes that the power of servant leadership is the power of asking and living in questions. "As a leader," he says, "I collect questions!" The two most powerful questions that inform his leadership are "Why are we here?" and "Where are we going?" Through these and other questions, Phil has shaped a distinct and successful leadership philosophy he calls "purposeful selfishness." To clarify this, he returns to Mandela's speech: "As we are liberated from our fear, our presence automatically liberates others." As a leader, he believes, he must work on liberating himself in order to hear his calling.

A primary role of the servant-leader is to answer the question many followers are asking today: "Why should I follow you?" Today, servant-leaders understand that all change is self-change; we really can't compel people to do anything. We can only encourage them to want to do things. They understand that real commitment and discretionary energy come through purpose.

As a coach to many leaders, I have been impressed with the hunger that great leaders have for some purpose higher than just personal career and financial success. They want to know clearly what they are leading for.

We yearn today for servant-leaders who are leading from within themselves. We yearn for leaders who lead with service and purpose. Purpose is something lived every day—it can be seen in what leaders do rather than what they say. It is embodied in the way a leader spends his or her time, growing out of the leader's daily purpose moments and practices.

"Generative Spirits": Guides to Finding Purpose

To reflect on your own sense of working on purpose, consider the following practice: read about how important purpose is. Read the teachings of prophets and saints whose writings have lasted for thousands of years. These wise elders must have captured a bit of truth, because their teachings have withstood the test of time. What is said about purpose in the Jewish Scriptures, the New Testament, the Quran, the Bhagavad-Gita, and the writings of Buddha and Confucius? These writings span a period of over four thousand years, and yet they align around the same message. How can they all be wrong, mistaken about the power of purpose?

It is also helpful to observe people who are "on purpose." They are usually easy to spot, and when you spot one you know it instantly. Purposeful people naturally attract others because of their presence. They simply have "generative spirits": people feel good in their presence. We don't always recall what they did or said, but we always remember how they made us feel.

One person who has inspired me personally with his purpose is Walter Mondale. I have lived in the same neighborhood as "Fritz" for fourteen years and have seen how he treats ordinary people. He is generous and genuine in his connections to each person he meets. He makes considerable effort to learn about you—what you're working on, what your hopes are. He gives his gifts generously to needy causes. He is also generous with his ideas, his advice, and his desire to serve. He embodies the best practices of a servant-leader.

One of my former teachers, Dr. Usarabudh Arya, taught me this: "As the flower unfolds, the bees come uninvited." That's Walter Mondale. His life is a testament to the wisdom of my teacher. How many former U.S. vice presidents have devoted their lives to being servant-leaders? And how many of them are eighty-six years old and still serving?

Look for purpose moments right now. Many people delay, saying that one day—when they are retired or more secure—they will give back with their time, talent, or treasure. But the feeling of security cannot be obtained by accumulating more wealth. Being generous, in fact, actually makes people feel richer and less in need of more wealth. It also makes them feel less dependent on their wealth for security. That is why we need to start being generous now, or we might never learn the value of generosity.

When we operate out of a spirit of generosity, we are enhanced spiritually and emotionally. And these benefits to spiritual and emotional maturity keep paying off because generosity changes us in positive ways. We like ourselves more, which causes others to respond more positively to us.

Who are the "generative spirits" in your life? How do they make you feel?

Part IV

Living on Purpose

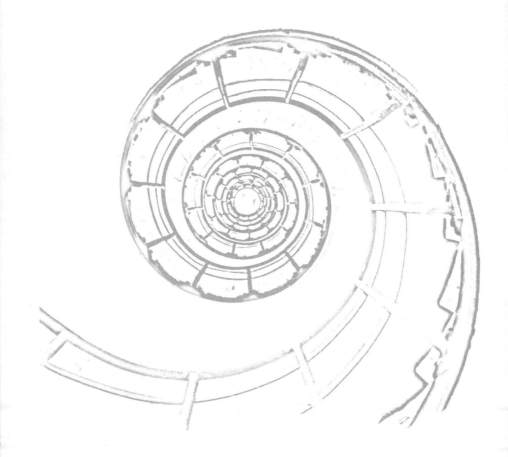

Chapter 10

Why Do I Get Up in the Morning?

Live the questions now. Perhaps then, someday far in the future, you will gradually, without even noticing it, live your way into the answer.
Rainer Maria Rilke

Living on purpose is a choice. It is a way of living in which you are aware each moment of each day that you have a choice about what to say and do and how to be. Every situation presents you with a new purpose moment—an opportunity to show up on purpose—and you are conscious of the opportunities.

In other words, living on purpose simply means becoming aware of who you are and what you are bringing to life during each day.

A good place to start living on purpose is to ponder the ultimate purpose question: Why do I get up in the morning? For many of us, this question is as tough as it is inevtable. Ideally, we should not let a day pass without spending some time reflecting on the question.

This chapter will explore answers to that question and discuss the link between purpose and happiness.

Live the Questions

Often we are so busy trying to answer the questions that we fail to take time to acknowledge, even celebrate, the questions themselves. We believe meaning comes from the answers, from knowing. In fact, our quest to know may make it harder to find meaning. We can so easily sit down at the computer and Google the answers that we rarely take the time to push the pause button and live in the questions, the big questions that matter. Technology has accelerated life, we are in a hurry, we have lost respect for the mystery embodied by the big questions.

In 1907, the German poet Rainer Maria Rilke wrote a letter to a young poet advising: "I would like to beg you, dear Sir, as well as I can, to have patience with everything unresolved in your heart and to try to love the questions themselves as if they were locked rooms or books written in a very foreign language. Don't search for the answers, which could not be given to you now, because you would not be able to live them. And the point is to live everything."[20]

First we need to ask ourselves what we need in our lives. A need is something we must have to survive. After we are clear about our basic needs, we can begin to look at our wants. Wants enrich the quality of our lives. And what we truly want often reflects our purpose.

Psychologist Abraham Maslow arranged human needs into a hierarchy.[21] He claimed that our basic needs must be at least minimally fulfilled before we can move toward our wants. Our physical needs (for example, air, food, shelter) are the most basic. These needs must be satisfied before we can free our energies to pursue needs at the next level. As Gandhi said, "Even God cannot talk to a hungry man except in terms of bread."

At the next level, according to Maslow, we must feel minimally safe and secure in our day-to-day activities. We all define safety and security in different ways, but the need to feel that our life and our work are rooted in solid ground is fundamental.

At the next level, we must feel a sense of companionship and affection. We need love—some kind of recognition that we have worth, that someone cares. Our self-worth can be badly damaged by the lack of real love. Self-worth will rise if we engage in life and work activities that we believe are worthwhile, in which we can be contributing members of society. To the extent that we spend our precious time on activities that we don't value, that we consider "worthless," our self-worth will diminish.

At the highest level, we need to operate with purpose. At this level we are growing, stretching, and utilizing our highest gifts and talents: we have a satisfying answer to the question, Why do I get up in the morning?

However, as Maslow added, "Even if all these needs are satisfied, we may still often (if not always) expect that a new discontent and restlessness will soon develop unless the individual is doing what he is fitted for. A musician must make music, an artist must paint, a writer must write if he is to be ultimately at peace with himself. What a [person] can be, [he or she] must be. This need we call self-actualization."

A frequent complaint that I hear in my coaching practice is a lack of meaning. Viktor Frankl called the feeling of emptiness, meaninglessness, or purposelessness the "existential vacuum." Such a state often results from the lack of a connection to something larger than and outside of ourselves.

Lack of Purpose Leads to "Inner Kill"

The existential vacuum is an attitude toward life held by too many people today. Take, for example, the vice president of a high-technology company whom I coach. "I just can't seem to get going," he said. "I used to be an up-and-coming executive with this company. Now I can't get interested in what I'm supposed to do. I know I should get rolling. I'm sleepwalking through the day. And I'm awake at night. I'm going to the liquor store twice a week when once used to be enough. I feel stuck!"

In short, he was struggling with "inner kill"—the art of dying without knowing it! He felt stuck in a kind of vocational quicksand. He was not challenged. He felt he could not leave, nor could he stay.

He went on to say, "I don't know how much longer I can last in this job. I've been with the company for fifteen years and have changed jobs every two to three years. The organization charts keep changing, but the politics don't. We're still being told what we must do and when. The old virtues of initiative and taking risks are not being rewarded. The process of getting rewards is more political now. I'm demoralized."

What was happening to this executive? He felt that no one cared about the contribution he was making. That caused him to raise the question What for?—as if he'd lost sight of his purpose for getting up in the morning.

Most people experience inner kill at some point in their lives. If a person is not challenged by meaningful tasks and is spared the positive stress surrounding such tasks, inner kill occurs. It is the condition of not having a compelling reason to get up in the morning.

Inner kill is similar to a garden in which nothing grows—it's empty. Life lacks purpose; nothing moves us. Our life lacks promise; it continues day after day at the same petty pace. Helen Keller said, "Life is either a daring adventure or nothing." That nothing is inner kill.

Like the more generalized depression, inner kill cuts across all ages and levels. People in these situations feel chronic fatigue, self-criticism, and anger or indifference. They can no longer invest themselves in others or in their work. Most of us recognize the phenomenon of being more or less awake on different days. With inner kill, our talents are always slumbering.

Once people reach the point of inner kill, they often find it difficult to see any other possibilities for themselves. Or they may not be able to decide which option to take.

The Drain of Indecision

Almost every person at some point in their life ponders, Which way to go? During each phase of our lives, we reflect on where we've been, where we're going, what we've accomplished, and what we still hope to do. We wonder whether to stay or leave a place, hang onto or let go of a relationship. At times we may feel like we've become fugitives from ourselves. We yearn for ways to overcome the drain of indecision and find opportunities to claim our maturity.

Some people are experiencing the pressures of life transitions and feel pulled in many directions—sandwiched between taking care of their children and their parents, dealing with divorce, remarriage, second families, blended families, empty nesting, widowhood, illness and recovery, and the list goes on.

At work, too, many people have reached a plateau and realize that their talents are not being fully used. They feel that they have outgrown their jobs, companies, or even their fields. Some feel bored. Others feel blocked by leaders who they feel simply don't understand them. One or a combination of these feelings can make a person dislike getting up to go to work.

Millions of people are stuck in the drain of indecision, struggling alone with why they should get up in the morning. The inability to be fully ourselves in what we do keeps us stuck in the indecision cycle. To recapture our vitality, we must be authentic—we must genuinely express our inner selves in the outer world.

What's It All About?

It occurred to psychologist Fred Kiel that he was losing his passion for his work. He was beginning to question why he was getting up and going to work in the morning. He was also questioning his stressful travel schedule. He says, "I was suddenly very hungry to see to it that all parts of my life hung together as one integrated whole."

He started the journey to wholeness when he was about

three years old. He recalls, "I can remember as a very young child being puzzled about human nature—and perhaps most of all puzzled about my own nature and experience. I had continually sought answers in a variety of ways from my parents and authority figures. My parents were loving and well-meaning people, but they rarely talked to me about the big questions."

From parents and authority figures, Fred turned next to "the god of our modern world—science." He turned away from heart to head and spent a couple of decades searching for meaning through biology and psychology. Eventually, he tired of that struggle and concluded that "the only real security in this life was to have financial independence."

That "dry hole" didn't last as long. Financial success didn't deliver either meaning or independence.

So, he began listening more deeply—listening to his clients, his friends, his wife, and his children. But most of all, he relates, "I've been listening to my heart, to quiet voices when I meditate, pray, and worship. I've been listening when I walk on our farmland. And I've been quietly led to seek wisdom and answers from the most unlikely places."

Fred became fascinated with and a student of the Amish culture. He claims that the Amish live by specific decision rules. Before the elders will embrace a new invention or accept a change, they must be convinced that the change both enhances and supports family and community life. Further, it must not harm the earth, as the Amish see themselves as stewards of the earth.

Studying and visiting the Amish has helped Fred "peel the layers of the onion to arrive at the heart," or more precisely, at his heart! From this point forward, Fred wants to live in ways similar to the Amish values. He wants his behavior to enhance his and others' family and community life and to have a low impact on the environment.

Living with these values in mind has helped Fred reshape a lot of his choices. It's no longer enough to just get up in the morning to make money as a psychologist. He states, "I still want to make money, but I now want to work on purpose. I want my professional behavior to meet my values. I want to work with clients who I know are in alignment with my purpose."

Fred's purpose each morning is simply this: "In all relationships I want to be a force to help people with matters of the heart." He believes that when people are grounded and live well from their hearts, they naturally tend to make choices that are good for family life, for community life, and for the environment.

Like the Amish, Fred's calling has a spiritual grounding. As he sums it up, "I want to devote the balance of my life to serving God as I have come to understand the divine." In the second half of the purpose journey, he feels at peace about many of the mysteries of life. He's concluded, "I don't need to understand any more about human nature than I already know, and I guess I don't understand it much more than I did at age three."

Every one of us, simply because we are human, periodically wonders, What am I here to do? Most major spiritual traditions — Buddhism, Hinduism, Judaism, Christianity, and Islam — deal with this question. We have to work at finding our authentic self and true calling. If we act from a false self—based on superficial values and outer success—we will always jump from one illusion to another. We will never be deeply happy.

Can Money Buy Happiness?

Researchers at the University of British Columbia, Vancouver, and Harvard Business School wondered if money really could make people happy. They theorized that how people spend their money might make a difference or even be as important as how much money people earn. Led by social psychologist Elizabeth Dunn, the researchers conducted a series of studies.[22]

First, they asked a nationally representative sample of more than six hundred thirty Americans to rate their general happiness, report their annual income, and provide a breakdown of their monthly spending, including bills, gifts for themselves, gifts for others, and donations to charity.

"Regardless of how much income each person made," Dunn reports, "those who spent money on others reported greater happiness, while those who spent more on themselves did not."

In another experiment the researchers gave $5 or $20 to participants, asking them to spend the money by 5 p.m. that day. Half the participants were instructed to spend the money on themselves (pay a bill or indulge in a treat), and half were assigned to spend the money on others (donate to charity or give a gift). Participants who spent the money on others reported feeling overwhelmingly happier at the end of the day than those who spent the money on themselves.

A corollary study was conducted with people spending their own money, and the results were consistent. The researchers also found that the amount of money, $5 or $20, was inconsequential.

So money *can* buy happiness—if you spend it on others!

Perhaps the biggest surprise in the study came when people were invited to predict the outcome of the experiment. Most thought that spending money on themselves would make them happier, but in fact the opposite was true—it is prosocial spending that makes people happy.

Are You Happy?

Most of us feel somewhat entitled to happiness, or at least we are curious about it. After all, the U.S. Declaration of Independence clearly states, "We hold these truths to be self-evident, that all [people] are created equal, that they are endowed by their Creator with certain unalienable rights, that among these are life, liberty and the pursuit of happiness."

Despite an almost universal belief to the contrary, the pursuit of happiness as it is interpreted today is a myth. Ease, comfort, and a state of having arrived do not constitute happiness for most human beings.

The fact is that satisfaction always leads to dissatisfaction! A life without intention and purpose leads to a sparse and shallow existence. Comfort and leisure are great, but they're just not enough. If this were the case, the large number of us who enjoy relative affluence would be ecstatically happy!

So what is this thing called happiness? People frequently

claim to define it, but others conclude that individuals must define happiness for themselves. What's more, happiness is always changing. Or is it? Is happiness fame, power, money? Is it marriage, family, community? Is it self-awareness, mindfulness, enlightenment? Is it doing work you love, painting a picture, or creating something beautiful? Or is it all of the above? And will it be the same tomorrow—will your happiness last?

Happiness is now considered a legitimate subject for academic study as well as research. More than two hundred colleges and universities, including Harvard, where I lecture, offer courses in positive psychology with a focus on happiness. Positive psychologist Martin Seligman has proposed that we all have an "emotional baseline—a level of happiness" to which we almost inevitably return.

According to Sonja Lyubomirsky, psychology professor and author of *The How of Happiness,* one's happiness level is determined by three things: 50 percent by one's emotional baseline, 10 percent by one's life circumstances, and 40 percent by "intentional activity."[23] She coined the phrase "40 percent solution": you can boost your happiness by 40 percent if you engage in intentional activities.

In short, happiness is the pursuit of living an intentional life with a reason to get up in the morning. Yet for every person who summons up the energy and courage to ask, Why do I get up in the morning? there are many others who hope that more busyness will feed their hunger.

Stop for a moment and ask yourself, Why do I get up in the morning? Repeat the question several times out loud. Does your answer satisfy you?

Chapter 11

How Do I Stay on Purpose?

To everything there is a season, and a time to every purpose under heaven:
. . . a time to weep, and a time to laugh; a time to mourn, and a time to
dance.

Ecclesiastes 3:1, 4

Staying on purpose through the busy routines of work and life is not easy. Our daily routine often lacks a sense of "why?" Life may appear to have no purpose, to serve no apparent ends.

Thus, we are in great need of deliberate reminders of the "why." Yet we create little time for regular relaxation and reflection. It is through open, focused reflection that we see beneath the surface to the place where we know not with the mind but with the heart. Here our intuitive side recognizes a power beyond the natural and rational, and we are able to accept the unknown on faith.

There are steps we can take to enhance our ability to think quietly and calmly and to open our listening. This chapter suggests two tools that will help you reflect, listen, and stay on purpose: regular times alone, or "solos," and starting a purpose study group.

But first, I want to look at the costs of not using such tools to keep us focused on our purpose.

The Problem: Hurry Sickness

Whenever I bring up the topics of reflection, solitude, and listening in my workshops or coaching, I usually get the response, "Who has time? I'm too busy!" That is a symptom of the problem. Busyness is crowding out our awareness of what is happening in and to our lives. Our very sense of humanity—our full-bodied presence in our lives—is being hijacked by hurry sickness. Symptoms include always rushing somewhere else, never being conscious of being anywhere; always doing, never contemplating what we are doing and why; and not being clear about why we get up in the morning.

This situation was brought home clearly in a provocative YouTube video sent to me recently, "No Time to Think,"[24] by David Levy, a professor in the Information School at the University of Washington. The video offers a disturbing wake-up call, showing how American society has become enslaved to an ethic of "more-better-faster" and is losing touch with the capacity for reflection and being present.

Levy's research focuses on why the technological devices (such as my Blackberry!) that are designed to connect us also seem to powerfully disconnect us. It appears that although our society supposedly prizes creativity and innovative thought, it in fact gives little credence to intuition and contemplative practices. Twitter may be the next level of connection, but surely there is something strange and ironic about the popularity of twittering as our human moments of present time dwindle.

Instead of connecting us, our communication technologies are isolating us, until isolation has become the norm. E-mail, voicemail, instant messaging, cell phones, text messaging, Facebook, Twitter, and of course the World Wide Web all serve useful roles. But these tools for connecting also crowd out deeper, face-to-face connections in our relationships and add to the level of busyness we perceive.

According to Thomas Eriksen of the University of Oslo, author of *Tyranny of the Moment*, the digital environment favors "fast-time" activities—those that require instant, urgent responses. Such activities tend to take precedence over and shut out "slow-time" activities, such as reflection, play, and "courageous (deep) conversations."[25] The right-now is trumping the timeless—high tech is hijacking the high-touch communication that we desperately need to be present to others and to ourselves. This is a major loss, and we are becoming overwhelmed and tired in the process.

Recovering Alone: Taking a "Solo"

One important way to recover from hurry sickness and refocus on our purpose is to plan regular times for solitude—"solos" during which we can be quiet and not distracted by the usual busyness. Hearing a calling requires regular periods of silence. As we take regular solos, we begin unmasking illusions. Slowly we start discerning what parts of our busyness are expressions of our real purpose.

When we get out of touch with our core, we lose our life perspective. We gain back our energy and focus by solitude—and by letting our reflective insights guide our day-to-day decisions. Solitude enhances our focus and taps our deep energy.

Sometimes we are receptive to solitude; at other times we are not. When crises drop into our lives, we are forced to reflect. At times when things seem to be going smoothly, we may not sense the need at all. Yet our intuition contracts silently from lack of use.

For many of us, solitude may seem strange or difficult, yet a solo can help us see and appreciate our entire life pattern. But what is a solo? Soloing is simply a process of sitting quietly, taking three deep breaths, and listening.

"How do I take a solo?" First of all, take three deep breaths! In the morning, for instance, get up a little earlier, and before you get involved in anything, just sit quietly and take three deep breaths. Then focus on your day ahead. Picture yourself moving through an ideal day of purpose moments. An architect first has an idea or a plan, then designs a building. An artist often has a similar inspiration. Think of your solo as time to create a blueprint for your day.

Some people prefer to take a solo every day. Some are more inclined to go to a quiet place to reflect weekly or monthly. Others create solo time when they're driving long distances, walking, jogging, listening to music, praying, or meditating.

Ideally, we should not let a day pass without spending some solo time listening. Eventually we really start uncovering our deepest selves. The solo is a practice to help us stay on purpose.

Solitude and relaxation both play important roles in reflection. In a quiet, relaxed state, we find it easier to concentrate our attention in the direction we choose and to develop a clearer perception of the purpose moments in our lives. Try this ten-minute solo exercise:

- Sit in a comfortable position. Consciously examine your physical tension and describe it to yourself in detail. Examine its intensity. Become as aware as you possibly can of any tension and related discomfort. Tighten up the tense area, then relax it. If you touch the tense area with your hand, you will feel the discomfort. Interesting areas to try are your jaw, back, neck, and eye muscles. Most people are tense in these areas without being fully aware of it.

- Close your eyes. Take three slow, deep breaths, breathing from your abdomen. Breathe in and out through your nose, taking breaths that are long and slow. Silently count "one" as you inhale and "two" as you exhale. Do this over and over again for several minutes. Concentrate on the numbers one and two, saying them to yourself for each breathing cycle. The idea is to clear your mind. Most of us feel controlled by thoughts that constantly pop into our minds. Visualize your thoughts as clouds floating toward you, floating freely into your mind, and then floating out of your mind again. Keep going back to counting your breaths. Clearing your mind will become easier as you practice.

- After you have enjoyed the quiet for several minutes, spend three to four minutes picturing your day as ideal, happening just as you want it to. You might want to ask: Why am I getting up this morning? What calls forth my gifts? What moves me? Where do I see myself serving?

- Keeping the pictures in your mind, affirm silently to yourself, "I will make a difference in one person's life today." Picture who that person might be. To affirm means to "make firm" that which you are picturing. If doubts or contradictory thoughts arise, don't resist them; just let them flow through your mind, and return to your images.

- Don't be in a hurry to open your eyes. Before you do, suggest to yourself that you are getting more and more alert — that you will feel clear and calm when you return.

As you see, the solo process is relatively simple. Using it really effectively, however, requires consistent practice.

If we are sincere in our intention to stay on purpose, we will soon find that the solo experience will become easier and more natural, and we will look forward to being by ourselves. "What we brood over, hatches out!" What this means from a practical standpoint is that we always attract into our lives whatever we think about the most, believe in most strongly, or expect on the deepest levels. Try it daily for a week with an open mind and heart, and then judge whether it is useful.

If we continue using and developing the solo habit, the changes in ourselves and in our sense of purpose will become an integral part of our lives and our days. Our awareness will become continuous, a state of "purposeful moments." The solo is one of the most powerful tools we have at our disposal. Our mindfulness determines the power of our purpose.

Have you created a space to provide "solo" time in your life for reflection?

Recovering with Others: Starting a Purpose Study Group

Another way to stay on purpose is to start a Purpose Study Group to enjoy exploring *The Power of Purpose* and the pleasure of each other's company. The book serves as a catalyst for thoughtful inquiry and staying on purpose, and sometimes people find it easier to begin a process if they can discuss progress with others.

The Purpose Study Group is patterned after a group that Benjamin Franklin established in 1727. His group, called the Junto, met every Friday night in a room over a tavern in Philadelphia. Franklin claimed the club was "the best School of Philosophy, Morals and Politics that then existed in the Province." Every meeting opened with a set of "queries" (both pious and practical) with a pause between questions, when one might fill and sip a glass of wine. The Junto endured thirty years; Franklin even thought of making it international.[26]

To start a group, ask two or more people to join you. Try to enlist people with one or more of the following qualifications: they are interested in exploring the topic of purpose; you feel comfortable talking openly with them; they will agree to meet with you on a regular basis; they will read the book and answer selected questions before each meeting; and they feel comfortable with dialogue.

Purpose Study Group meetings can be held around breakfast or lunch, after work, or any time that people can commit to two hours of discussion. Some process suggestions include:

- Meet four times.

- Meet once a week for a month, twice a month for two months, or once a month for four months.

- Plan to meet for two hours.

- Designate a facilitator for each meeting to help the flow of discussion.

- Members should complete the specific reading and reflection assignments (see *The Purpose Study Group* in Resources at the back of the book) before each meeting.

Who might you invite to join you in a Purpose Study Group?

Chapter 12

How Do I Live Longer, Better?

Through compassion, you find that all human beings are just like you.
The Dalai Lama

We are born as purpose-seeking creatures. Purpose is necessary for our very health and longevity. If you doubt this, check out the rates of illness and death when people lose or give up their sense of purpose. People who retire without something to retire to have a much higher incidence of early mortality and illness than do those who have a focus.

Research is beginning to validate what many people have known intuitively all along: when it comes to longevity and well-being, purpose is working in our favor. A sense of meaning grows out of the choices that we make moment to moment. Meaning develops as we experience these purpose moments in life. And meaning deepens with spiritual evolution. When we clarify and settle on an intentional purpose in life, we often find a spiritual home, and a greater sense of well-being arises in our moment-to-moment, day-to-day actions in the world.

This chapter will help you see the connection between meaning and both longevity and well-being.

The Vitality Project

The citizens of Albert Lea, Minnesota, conducted an experiment to measurably improve the health of their entire community. Rather than promoting diet and exercise messages, which fail for most people, the Vitality Project implemented lessons from the "Blue Zones"—the longevity hot spots around the world. Led by National Geographic global explorer Dan Buettner, who authored the best-selling book *The Blue Zones*,[27] and Joel Spoonheim, the creative project director, a team of committed public servants and community volunteers implemented the most innovative and comprehensive makeover of an entire town ever undertaken in U.S. history.

The AARP/Blue Zones Vitality Project, sponsored by United Health Foundation, implemented the nine "lessons from the people who live the longest," detailed in Buettner's book. The Blue Zones approach was to set up four environments of community life to support healthy choices, including the following criteria: Is the town easy to walk and bike through? Are friends supportive? Are homes and offices set up to make healthy choices easy? Do we wake up with a sense of purpose?

The project's goal was to transform the environments of people's lives to increase longevity by an average of two years per person. National experts (including me) were brought in to teach participants about best practices. Around 25 percent of the adult population of the community participated through over a dozen concurrent initiatives implemented during just ten months.[28] Participants took an online Vitality Compass® quiz at the beginning and end of the project. The quiz at the end of the project showed projected longevity increases of 2.9 years!

Cathy and Kevin Purdie attended a workshop on Finding Your Purpose. Cathy was already very committed to improving the town by convincing more than two-thirds of restaurants to offer healthier choices. But in this workshop, these busy working parents uncovered a shared vision to be better role models for their children. They found that this could be done best by finishing their college degrees, which they started working on weeks later. When I visited with the Purdies at the project's completion celebration, they introduced me to their beaming children, who were obviously proud of their parents' decisions to finish their educations. Kevin said, "A clear sense of purpose was the essential tool that got us going, and it is essential for any person striving for a healthy life."

Nearly a thousand people (seven percent of the adult population) attended purpose workshops, resulting in 2,276 volunteer hours logged and the launch of a new volunteer-matching Web site. The increased "purpose moments" are harder to measure, but the mood of service and community is palpable. Community is not only a place but also a state of mind, and that mindfulness begins from within. It begins with hope, a sense of what's possible, a commitment to a cause, a yearning to solve a problem, or a restless need to express one's creativity in service to the community.

The project, as planned, created a replicable model that received extensive national media attention. Because of the exceptional coverage, requests for similar projects are coming from around the country. As the citizens of towns across the country realign internal and external environments, they will find that healthy, purposeful choices become easy choices.

The Purpose Project

With the upsurge of worldwide interest in the connection between spiritual beliefs and practices and health, practitioners of modern medicine are researching the relationship between meaning and health and longevity. More and more studies are indicating that when we are connected to something larger than ourselves, we strengthen our ability to cope with life's challenges.

No one knows exactly how spiritual beliefs and practices affect health. Some experts attribute the healing effect to hope, which has been shown to benefit our immune system. Others point to our social connectedness.

However, a growing body of research and practice suggests that people who feel that their life is part of a larger plan have stronger immune systems, lower blood pressure, a lower risk of heart attack and cancer, plus they live longer—seven years on average—than those without such a belief. When we believe in something larger than ourselves, we also strengthen our capacity to cope with life's challenges and transitions. One result of this research and practice has been an enormous increase in the number of U.S. medical schools that teach courses on spirituality and healing— from 3 in the mid-1990s to 72 of 125 medical schools now.[29]

The University of Minnesota's Center for Spirituality and Healing,* which is part of the Academic Health Center, enriches health and well-being through education, research, and innovative programs that advance integrative health and healing. The timing was just right when the center's pioneering founder and director, Mary Jo Kreitzer, invited me to become a Senior Fellow. Together we would create the Purpose Project to advance the understanding of how meaning was fundamental to health, healing, happiness, and ultimately, longevity.

The project has had an impact since day one. Our purpose—"creating a more healthy world through the power of purpose"—led us to sponsor the Second Annual Positive Aging Conference, with an emphasis on the role of purpose in aging and longevity. Through our Working on Purpose outreach workshops, we have offered thousands of people the time, tools, and framework to create a positive second-half-of-life plan. Our vision—"to lead the international purpose movement"—is taking hold.

The project's vision has also pushed my own growth edge and has brought a new depth, breadth, and vitality to my work practice, giving me renewed focus and revitalized energy.

Living on Purpose = Years of Healthy Life

We have discovered with both the Vitality Project and the Purpose Project that what most people really want is not just longevity—more years to live—but years that are vital and meaningful.

The U.S. Department of Health and Human Services publication *Healthy People 2010* describes a measure called

*www.csh.umn.edu

"years of healthy life,"[30] which is the difference between life expectancy and time spent with chronic or acute health limitations. According to government studies, in 1996 Americans lived an average 64.2 years of "healthy life."

Healthy life extends beyond the physical to include the emotional, social, and spiritual. This is everyone's ultimate goal, I believe—more years of healthy life. So what is the key to extending years of healthy life?

Medical researchers are only now beginning to understand the physiological consequences of expressing care and compassion. They report that we experience distinct physical sensations while we are helping. Some people describe these feelings as a "helper's high," saying they feel lighter and more energetic. Other people experience calmness and fewer aches and pains.

There is no evidence as yet that the physical and emotional sensations experienced by people who are helping others are a result of chemicals in the brain. However, it is known that chemicals called endorphins, the body's natural painkillers and mood enhancers, have the capacity to stimulate feelings similar to "helper's highs." It may turn out that doing good increases endorphins or other positive chemicals, and even that self-absorption may decrease the production of such chemicals. More research is certainly required.

Even without scientific evidence, though, people recognize that as they help others over time, as they feel they are truly making a difference in the world or in individual lives, the personal emotional "glow" becomes more widespread, leading to greater feelings of self-worth and a deeper sense of purpose. Even the memory of an act of giving can provide a lasting sense of satisfaction and meaning long after the helping act has been completed.

Living Better by Helping Others — Even If You Are Ill

People with acute or chronic illness are by no means excluded from experiencing the power of purpose. When our way of life is dramatically changed by illness or disability, as it was for marathon runner Terry Fox (see Chapter 2), the change not only forces us to reevaluate our lives and let go of previous ways of being but can stimulate a search for new sources of meaning.

Physical illness or disability may take away independence and make inaccessible those things that provided, or might have provided, purpose and meaning when we were healthier and more able. However, one of the great truths of purpose is that it is not limited by circumstances. In fact, major challenges may offer the choice of new directions and purpose that can add years of healthy life. As a result, we may experience a new calling to serve others in some way.

Unfortunately, the failure to reimagine purpose and direction in such situations can—and often does—result in depression, despair, and the drain of indecision.

As a young woman, Nancy Gunderson loved the outdoors and wilderness canoeing as much as the intellectually challenging world of archeological and historical research. Her plans included a career in museum administration, more European travel to use her four languages and research family genealogy, and to marry and have children.

Nancy's life contracted sharply when she came down with a debilitating illness in her late twenties. As her strength and energy drained and her pain level increased, she first gave up her plans for graduate school and dreams of having a family, then even her career. On full disability, unable to drive, for the last twenty years Nancy has depended on a care network of friends to do what she can no longer do for herself: shop for groceries, clean her condo, do her laundry, drive her to doctor appointments. Once comfortable traveling around Oslo, Frankfurt, and Paris on her own, Nancy is now limited to the hallways of her condo, which she travels in her electric wheelchair, or the occasional outing that friends provide.

Yet Nancy lives a life on purpose. She is an attentive and loving aunt to her three nephews who live three states away. It is beyond her ability to visit them, but she is still involved in their lives via Skype. The friends who shop, clean, and do her laundry always find wise counsel and encouragement, thoughtful gifts, and playful humor at her table over a cup of coffee. She watches out for her frail, elderly condo neighbors, whom she has befriended, and calls their family members when they need help. Still a whiz at leading book group meetings and probing financial reports, she volunteers as treasurer on her condo board, and although the effort leaves her bedridden for several days following each board meeting, she has managed to get budgeting for needed building maintenance on track.

Nancy may lack health, strength, and energy, but she finds meaning and well-being in caring for others as they care for her.

The purpose-filled person in an assisted-living facility,

nursing home, or other institutional setting may decide to give the gifts of listening and companionship by initiating conversations with other residents, offering time for listening, and, if needed, providing encouragement and hope. Serving in this way empowers people who are ill and gives them a reason to get up in the morning. As their lives take on new meaning, the body's natural healing mechanisms may be invigorated, and years of healthy life may be added.

Staying on Purpose

To stay on purpose, we need stress. Yes, you read that correctly. We all know that stress can be negative. In the United States, stress results in absenteeism and medical expenses that cost the economy two hundred billion dollars a year.[31] Stress can even be deadly. Obviously, we need less, not more, of that kind of stress.

What we need is the right amount of the right kind of stress. Not only too-great demands but also the opposite — the lack of purpose — may cause disease. However, a creative tension between what we have and what we want is a motivator.

Many would argue that serving or expressing goodwill toward others provides a needed positive stress. Hans Selye, the medical researcher who coined the term *stress*, has suggested that the way to enjoy a rewarding lifestyle free of disabling stress is to practice "altruistic egoism." In essence, this involves serving others.

Selye points out that our biological nature drives us toward self-preservation, or what might commonly be called selfishness. Selye's line of thought suggests that only by linking this self-centered innate nature with an attitude of earning the goodwill and respect of others through altruistic efforts will a happy, meaningful life result.

We may never fully understand our altruistic urge, let alone human nature, but the heart of purpose is centered in the simple idea of caring for our fellow human beings—and caring for ourselves in the process.

We can choose to make our caring for each other be what our lives are all about. The challenge is for us to discover what kind of caring provides that feeling of aliveness we seek.

What we need is creative tension between a person and a purpose he or she wants to fulfill. We are not searching for stress per se but rather are searching in particular for tasks whose completion will add meaning to our lives.

What do you feel when you help others or show compassion? Are you getting your "minimum daily requirements" of caring for others?

Chapter 13

What Is the Meaning of Life?

One should not search for an abstract meaning of life. Everyone has [his or her] own vocation or mission in life to carry out a concrete assignment, which demands fulfillment.

Viktor Frankl

From birth onward, we are all growing older, but are we also growing up, or maturing? Aging belongs to the body, and maturing belongs to the spirit. Aging requires nothing special from us; maturing requires a spiritual quest. Maturity is spiritual wisdom embodied.

We all long to grow in wisdom as well as in years, but unless we make conscious choices to do so, we may simply grow old. What keeps us from growing up? How is maturity gained? This chapter will explore those questions and discuss the vital links between wisdom, spirituality, and the meaning of life, and our purpose.

No Time for Spirituality

If we live as victims, without choosing, we simply become old. But when we age with conscious choice, we can walk the path of spiritual evolution and grow whole, mature, wise. These are the only two choices.

What stands in the way of choosing the spiritual path to wholeness and wisdom? Time. The number one pressure on people today is lack of time. Technology encourages us to be "on" twenty-four hours a day, seven days a week via computers, smart phones, and other devices. Electronic gadgets have done away with boundaries to work, making us available outside normal work hours, even on weekends and holidays and during vacations. For more and more of us, the workday never ends.

We have always had trouble with time. What's different today is that pervasive technology and a mindset that we must respond instantly have accelerated life and made it more intense. We find it ever harder to be present with ourselves and with others and to connect with a Higher Power.

As a result, our spirit—in particular, our spiritual maturity—suffers. We become spiritually numb, and a meaningful life falls by the wayside—a victim of our hurry sickness.

The Importance of Spirituality to Meaning

People often use the words *spirituality* and *religion* interchangeably, but they're not the same. Religion has more to do with following the practices and dictates of a tradition or institution, whereas spirituality is more personal, encompassing our personal relationship with a Higher Power.

The Spirituality in Healthcare Committee at Mayo Clinic offers the following definition: "Spirituality is a dynamic process by which one discovers inner wisdom and vitality that give meaning and purpose to all life events and relationships."[32]

The committee's report goes on to say that "spirituality as a dynamic process helps individuals discover meaning and purpose in their lives, even in the midst of personal tragedy, crisis, stress, illness, pain, and suffering. This process is an inner quest. This quest involves openness to the promptings of one's soul or spirit, silence, contemplation, meditation, prayer, inner dialogue and/or discernment. Spirituality empowers a person to be fully engaged in life experiences from birth to death."

To find meaning and live on purpose, we must feel connected and present—to ourselves, to others, to a Higher Power—and leave busyness by the wayside.

"Can You Tell Me What My Purpose in Life Is?"

Purpose has little to do with genius or gender, ethnicity or age. It is discovering what we truly care about. It is uncovering the gifts within us and giving them away. It is being thoroughly used up when we die because we gave it all away while we were living.

A young man who was searching for his life's purpose wrote to Rabbi Menachem Mendel Schneerson. He said he had discussed the purpose question with every wise person he had ever come across, had read every book on purpose he could find, and had traveled to faraway places to seek the guidance of some of the greatest spiritual teachers. However, no one had ever been able to tell him what his purpose was.

So he asked the rabbi, "Can you tell me what my purpose in life is?"

Rabbi Schneerson responded, "By the time you figure out what your mission is, you will have no time to fulfill it. So just get on with it." In other words, do more acts of goodness, and your life's purpose will unfold before you, one day at a time.

We can spend a lifetime philosophizing about the meaning of life, pondering our place in the universe, and miss out on the purpose moments.

The power of purpose means recognizing that we were given another day to live—today—and along with that we were given the choice to make a difference in at least one other person's life. A life of purpose moments is not self-absorbed soul-searching. It is simply opening our eyes with caring and compassion. Who around us needs a hand? How can we improve the little corner of the planet we live on? What can we do, this very moment, to make a small difference in someone's life?

Discovering personal purpose is a cradle-to-grave journey. As we mature, our purpose becomes deeper, richer, and more moment-to-moment. Purpose begins with the genuine desire to connect with the greatest good within ourselves and others. Charles Handy, in *The Age of Paradox,* wrote: "True fulfillment is, I believe, vicarious. We get our deepest satisfaction from the fulfillment and growth and happiness of others. It takes time, often a lifetime, to realize this. Parents know it well, as do teachers, great managers, and all who care for the downtrodden and unfortunate."[33]

Seeing the Pattern of Life

If we are to have a livable, sustainable world for the twenty-first century, purpose, compassion, and care for others must become our guiding ethos. We each need to strengthen our core capacity for compassion not only to help sustain the world but also to foster our own well-being.

As we saw in Chapter 12, purpose moments enhance physical and emotional well-being and improve our longevity. For instance, a study by psychologist David McClelland found that people who simply watched a film of Mother Teresa providing care for the poor in India enjoyed significant positive changes in their immune function.[34] We can speculate, then, that ignoring the needs of others and focusing entirely on ourselves is likely to have the opposite effect on our immune systems.

On our path toward purpose, our sense of the larger spiral pattern evolves. The more mature we are, the more likely we are to see the pattern. We see the pattern we missed earlier in our lives. We see the interconnectedness of our lives and the lives of others in the world. We see that the larger pattern includes all people, all cultures, and all religions on the planet.

Knowing who we are at our core—what our voice is—and fully expressing our music enrich our journey. Whether our purpose is to serve God, to raise healthy children, to create a healthier environment, or to play beautiful music, we are empowered by our purpose.

We may not always see the results our lives have on others, but we can know deep down that we are making some contribution, large or small, to the larger pattern of life. We can know that we make a difference, that our life matters.

The Center of a Meaningful Life: Compassion

As we work our way toward the purpose of our lives, and find that helping others is more satisfying than indulging our own wants, we begin to understand that compassion is at the very center of a life lived on purpose. Compassion is the spiritual essence of purpose, requiring some connection with a Higher Power. All major religions have understood this and have taught the principle that we are to love and care for our neighbors, in contrast to focusing on our own needs and wants.

Consider what the great sages, prophets, and poets through the ages have said:

Moses (circa 1400 BC): "Do not seek revenge or bear a grudge against one of your people, but love your neighbor as yourself."
                                                                Leviticus 19:18

Krishna (900 BC): "One who engages in full devotional service, who does not fall down under any circumstances, at once transcends the modes of maternal nature and thus comes to the level of Brahman."
                                                          Bhagavad-Gita 14:26

Gautama Buddha (563–483 BC): "Consider others as yourself."
                                                              Dhammapada 10:1

Confucius (551–479 BC): "He who wishes to secure the good of others has already secured his own."

Jesus of Nazareth (AD 0–32): "Love your neighbor as yourself."

Matthew 19:19; "Do unto others as you would have them do to you."
                                                                   Luke 6:31

Muhammad (AD 570–632): "Whatever good ye give, shall be rendered back to you, and ye shall not be dealt with unjustly."
                                                                  Sura 2:272

A life centered on compassion is lived to further a purpose. It may be difficult or take what seems like a long time to determine our precise larger purpose, but compassion will set us on the path of discovery.

What Is Your "Concrete Assignment"?

Our Creator has given us free will to cocreate our destiny, but it is up to us to listen for the call and to choose to carry out our "concrete assignment," as Frankl put it. That concrete assignment is a call to serve. It's a spiritual call—a nudge—from a loving Creator who wants His creatures to fulfill their purpose on earth. Accomplishing the purpose for which we were created may be the most important concrete task that many of us have remaining.

As our purpose evolves over our lifetime—as it is uncovered, discovered, and rediscovered—it gives our lives dignity and meaning. We are no longer burdened by compassion and purpose as a sense of duty or moral obligation: we care because it is our reason for being here.

The power of purpose is the power of compassion. It alone is the greatest of all the gifts we have to offer—our "concrete assignment."

Do Something About It

The original unpublished title of Frankl's classic book, *Man's Search for Meaning*, was *In Spite of Everything, Say Yes to Life*. His powerful point of view was put to the test on September 11, 2001.

Tom Burnett, a passenger on United Flight 93, called his

wife from the hijacked plane, aware by then that two other planes had crashed into the World Trade Center.[35]

"I know we're going to die," he said. "But some of us are going to do something about it." On that tragic morning, he did indeed do something about it. And because he did, many other lives were spared. His purpose moment continues to inspire us to, as Frankl suggests, "let life question us." What would we have done in a similar situation?

"I know we're going to die" is almost a matter-of-fact statement. Every day we each might think the same thought. But the deep lesson from Tom Burnett is in his second sentence: "But some of us are going to do something about it."

That sentence is the fundamental message of this book. We were all born for a reason. We are all going to die. So what are we going to do about it? The book's thesis is that a meaningful life comes from answering the call—from our own realization that the time has come to say yes to life and, ultimately, to "do something about it." Those words convey the fundamental challenge put to us by life.

The question is not what is the meaning of life, but who are we bringing to life? And the answer must be chosen by each of us every day in our own way, because a meaningful life always begins from within, from our choices. Meaning is uncovered in the day-to-day purpose moments when courage and compassion trump convenience. Meaning can be found in the listening presence of a friend, the outstretched hand of a stranger, the extra mentoring of a teacher, or daring to take a seat at the front of the bus.

Purpose moments are all around us. The power to do something about it is deep in our nature. Matching the two is this book's purpose—and the key to a meaningful life.

Resources

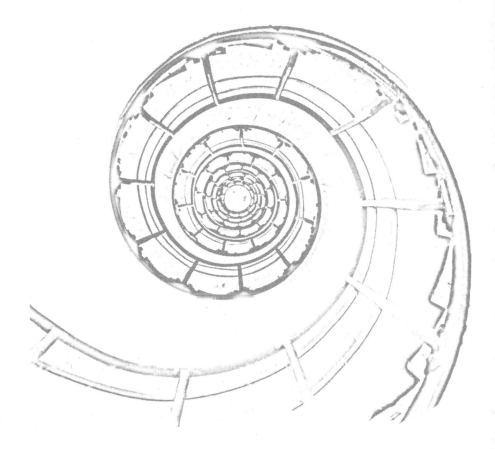

The Purpose Study Group

Session 1: The Meaning of Purpose

Read: The Preface and Part I, Chapters 1–4.

Do: Before the session, answer the following questions:

If you could live your life over again, what would you do differently? (Preface)

Look ahead. How old do you think you'll live to be? (Chapter 1)

My calling in life is _____. (Chapter 4)

Discuss: Decide who will be the facilitator.

Perform group introductions.

Read the quote by Andrew Greeley in Chapter 5 ("It seems to me that in the last analysis there are only two choices....") aloud and discuss it.

Discuss the three presession questions (above).

Session 2: Paths to Purpose

Read: Part II, Chapters 5–7.

Do: Review the eight intelligences in Chapter 6.

Rank-order yourself from 1 to 8 based on what you perceive your natural strengths to be (1 is highest, 8 is lowest).

Think of a talent that would fit in your #1 area.

Review the nine passion questions in Chapter 7.

Discuss: Read aloud the quote by Viktor Frankl at the beginning of Chapter 5 ("We can discover the meaning of life in three different ways . . .") and discuss it.

Discuss the eight intelligences in Chapter 6.

Compare the top three choices of group members.

Discuss the nine passion questions in Chapter 7.

Compare responses to the question, What moves you?

Ask each member to summarize his or her purpose journey (about five minutes).

Discuss the purpose spiral in Chapter 3.

Which phase do you see yourself in?

What is your core question?

Session 3: Working on Purpose

Read: Part III, Chapters 8 and 9.

Do: Before the session, answer the following questions:

             What are your expectations of work?

             Is work something to be suffered through and endured or is work synonymous with a calling?

Discuss: Read the Working-on-Purpose Inventory in the Resources at the end of the book, and discuss whether you feel the power of purpose at work.

             Read the quote from Marianne Williamson in Chapter 9 ("Our deepest fear is not that we are inadequate. . . .") aloud and discuss it.

Session 4: Living on Purpose

Read: Part IV, Chapters 10–13.

Do: Before the session, answer the following question: Why do I get up in the morning? (Chapter 10)

Discuss: Read the quote from Abraham Maslow in Chapter 10 ("Even if all these needs are satisfied . . .") aloud and discuss it.

Celebrate!

Core Questions on the Life Spiral

As we move through different phases in our life spiral, different core questions emerge. Purpose helps us live in the questions that are meaningful and life enhancing.

Middlessence:
What's calling
me next?

Young adulthood:
What is my
calling?

Young older adulthood:
How do I grow whole,
not old?

Elderhood:
What's my
legacy?

Birth

Childhood:
Who am I?

Adolescence:
What do I want to
be when I grow up?

The Purpose Checkup

After a certain age, many of us accept the necessity of regular physical checkups. We're also generally willing to review our financial situation with some regularity.

So if money, medicine, and meaning are all essential to a purposeful life, we might be wise to take guidance from the financial and medical worlds and adopt the practice of a regular checkup on that third dimension to ensure that our spirit—our sense of purpose—remains healthy.

Please read each statement carefully and take a few moments to decide on a true response for yourself. Then write the number that most nearly reflects that response. The answers offer the following range of responses:

1. Definitely disagree. 3. Somewhat agree.
2. Somewhat disagree. 4. Definitely agree.

Having (Outer Life)

_____ I derive satisfaction from what I have in my life.

_____ I express my creativity in a number of ways.

_____ I have found ways to offer my gifts and talents to the world.

_____ I have a positive vision for my future.

_____ I feel satisfied with my location.

_____ My physical energy is vital.

_____ I feel satisfied with my personal relationships.

_____ *Total Having score*

Doing (Inner Life)

_____ I follow my purpose when making major decisions.

_____ I feel content when I am alone.

_____ I focus and think clearly.

_____ I have the courage to face my adversities.

_____ I offer compassion to others readily.

_____ I offer forgiveness to others easily.

_____ I am growing and developing.

_____ *Total Doing score*

Being (Spiritual Life)

_____ I sense the presence of a Higher Power.

_____ I have a regular spiritual practice.

_____ I feel a sense of the sacred when I am in the natural world.

_____ I feel a sense of gratitude for my life.

_____ I maintain a balance of saving and savoring the world.

_____ I invest time in making a difference to others or to the world.

_____ I know what I want to be remembered for.

_____ *Total Being score*

_____ **Total Purpose Checkup score**

Interpretation

Having (Outer Life)

The dimension of your external experience and activity—how effectively you relate to the "having" choices in your life.

Doing (Inner Life)

The dimension of your internal experience and inner activity—how effectively you relate to the "doing" choices in your life.

Being (Spiritual Life)

The dimension of your invisible experience and spiritual activity—how effectively you relate to the "being" choices in your life.

Scoring

Your score in each section is one measure of your development in that dimension. Your total Purpose Checkup score (out of 84) gives a measure of the power of purpose you are experiencing in your life at present.

Use this checkup to check in with yourself yearly, perhaps on your birthday!

The Working-on-Purpose Inventory

Check yes or no according to how you feel about each question today.

	Yes	No
Do I wake up most Mondays feeling energized to go to work?	☐	☐
Do I have deep energy—feel a personal calling—for my work?	☐	☐
Am I clear about how I measure my success as a person?	☐	☐
Do I use my gifts to add real value to people's lives?	☐	☐
Do I work with people who honor the values I value?	☐	☐
Can I speak my truth in my work?	☐	☐
Am I experiencing true joy in my work?	☐	☐
Am I making a living doing what I most love to do?	☐	☐
Can I speak my purpose in one clear sentence?	☐	☐
Do I go to sleep most nights feeling this was a well-lived day?	☐	☐

Total yes responses: _____

The total number of yes responses on the inventory provides a general idea of your power of purpose at work. If you have many yeses, you're obviously intent on making a difference through your work. You probably have a sense of purpose or direction, but you might consider further clarifying your gifts, passions, and values.

Recommended Reading

Armstrong, Thomas. *7 Kinds of Smart.* New York: Plume, 1993.

Bateson, Mary Catherine. *Composing a Life.* New York: Plume, 1990.

Block, Peter. *Stewardship: Choosing Service over Self-Interest.* San Francisco: Berrett-Koehler, 1993.

Bolles, Richard. *How to Find Your Mission in Life.* Berkeley, CA: Ten Speed Press, 1991.

Bolles, Richard. *What Color Is Your Parachute?* Berkeley, CA: Ten Speed Press, 1997.

Bridges, William. *Transitions.* Reading, MA: Addison-Wesley, 1980.

Csikszentmihalyi, Mihalyi. *Flow: The Psychology of Optimal Experience.* New York: Harper & Row, 1990.

Fox, Matthew. *The Reinvention of Work: A New Vision of Livelihood for Our Time.* New York: HarperCollins, 1995.

Frankl, Viktor. *Man's Search for Meaning.* New York: Pocket Books, 1977.

Frankl, Viktor. *The Unheard Cry for Meaning.* New York: Touchstone, 1978.

Gardner, Howard. *Frames of Mind: The Theory of Multiple Intelligences.* New York: Basic Books, 1985.

Greenleaf, Robert. *Servant Leadership: A Journey into the Nature of Legitimate Power and Greatness.* New York: Paulist Press, 1977.

Leider, Richard J. *Claiming Your Place at the Fire: Living the Second Half of Your Life on Purpose.* San Francisco: Berrett-Koehler, 2004.

Leider, Richard J. *Something to Live For: Finding Your Way in the Second Half of Life.* San Francisco: Berrett-Koehler, 2008.

Leider, Richard J. *Whistle While You Work: Heeding Your Life's Calling.* San Francisco: Berrett-Koehler, 2001.

Leider, Richard J., and Shapiro, David. *Repacking Your Bags: Lighten Your Load for the Rest of Your Life.* San Francisco: Berrett-Koehler, 1995.

Murphy, Pat, and Neill, William. *By Nature's Design.* San Francisco: Chronicle Books, 1993.

Whyte, David. *The Heart Aroused: Poetry and the Preservation of the Soul in Corporate America.* New York: Currency/Doubleday, 1994.

Zambucka, Kristin. *Ano Ano: The Seed.* Honolulu: Mana Publishing, 1984.

The Purpose Path

Reading a book can be very helpful on the path to purpose, and I hope that this book has been useful to you in pursuing yours.

In this book, I have shared what I have learned from many wise teachers and life stories. I invite you to participate in an ongoing conversation "on purpose." If anything in this book touched you, troubled you, or inspired you, please write to tell me. I am interested in hearing about sources, resources, and stories of people living and working "on purpose." I'll respond.

You can travel the purpose path with products and pro-grams offered by the Inventure Group of Minneapolis. The Inventure Group, of which I am founder and a partner, is a coaching and consulting firm devoted to helping individuals, leaders, and teams discover the power of purpose.

The Inventure Group offers:

- Coaching for people on the purpose path.
- Keynote speeches for conferences and meetings.
- Workshops for leaders and teams focusing on leading on purpose.
- The Purpose online store with books, booklets, tools, and resources.
- Purpose expeditions to Africa.

If you wish further information about speeches, coaching, workshops, materials, or expeditions, please contact:

The Inventure Group

www.inventuregroup.com

www.richardleider.com

Notes

1. For more information about this study, visit www. MatureMarketInstitute.com.
2. O. Carl Simonton, "The Healing Journey" (lecture, Denver, 1996).
3. Terry Fox (1958–1981) was a Canadian humanitarian, athlete, and cancer treatment activist. He is considered one of Canada's greatest heroes—in a public opinion poll he was voted the most famous Canadian of the twentieth century. For more information, see www.terryfox.com.
4. Pat Murphy and William Neill, *By Nature's Design* (San Francisco: Chronicle Books, 1993).
5. Mary Catherine Bateson, *Composing a Life* (New York: Plume, 1990).
6. Peter Drucker, interview, *Psychology Today*, October 1968.
7. Ernest Becker, *The Denial of Death* (New York: Free Press, 1973).
8. Albert Schweitzer, *Peace or Atomic War?* (New York: Henry Holt and Company, 1958).
9. Sigurd F. Olson, *Open Horizons* (New York: Knopf, 1969).
10. The full quotation is "Many people die with their music still in them. Why is this so? Too often it is because they are always getting ready to live. Before they know it, time runs out."
11. Phillip L. Berman, *The Courage of Conviction* (New York: Dodd, Mead, 1985).
12. Richard Gregg, quoted in Duane Elgin, *Voluntary Simplicity: Toward a Way of Life That Is Outwardly Simple, Inwardly Rich*, rev. ed. (New York: Quill, 1998).
13. Howard Gardner, *Multiple Intelligences. New Horizons* (New York: Basic Books, 2006).
14. For more information, visit www.inventuregroup.com.
15. Mihalyi Csikszentmihalyi, *Flow: The Psychology of Optimal Experience* (New York: Harper & Row, 1990).
16. Matthew Fox, *The Reinvention of Work: A New Vision of Livelihood for Our Time* (New York: HarperCollins, 1995).
17. Juliet B. Schor, *The Overworked American: The Unexpected Decline of Leisure* (New York: Basic Books, 1991).
18. James A. Autry, *Love and Work: A Manager's Search for Meaning* (New York: Morrow, 1994).
19. Marianne Williamson, *A Return to Love: Reflections on the Principles of "A Course in Miracles"* (New York: HarperCollins, 1992).

20. Rainer Maria Rilke, *Letters to a Young Poet,* trans. Franz Xaver Kappus, intro. Reginald Snell (New York: Random House, 1984).

21. Deborah C. Stephens, ed., *The Maslow Business Reader* (New York: John Wiley, 2000).

22. Elizabeth W. Dunn, "A Policy of Happiness," *UBC Reports* 55, no. 1 (January 8, 2009).

23. Sonia Lyubomirsky, *The How of Happiness: A Scientific Approach to Getting the Life You Want* (New York: Penguin, 2008).

24. David M. Levy, "No Time to Think," video of a presentation at Google, http://www.youtube.com/watch?v=KHGcvj3JiGA.

25. Thomas Hylland Eriksen, *Tyranny of the Moment: Fast and Slow Time in the Information Age* (London: Pluto Press, 2001).

26. Franklin describes the formation of the Junto, also known as the Leather Apron Club, in his autobiography, *The Private Life of the Late Benjamin Franklin,* written in French and first published in English in 1793. I created my own Junto based on Franklin's model.

27. Dan Buettner, *The Blue Zones: Lessons for Living Longer from the People Who've Lived the Longest* (Washington, DC: National Geographic, 2008).

28. Approximately twenty-three hundred citizens of Albert Lea participated in the Vitality Project from January to October 2009. See www.aarp.org and www.bluezones.com for more information.

29. Edward Creagan, ed., *The Mayo Clinic Plan for Healthy Aging* (Mayo Clinic Health Information, 2006).

30. U.S. Department of Health and Human Services, *Healthy People 2010,* vols. 1 and 2 (Washington, DC: U.S. Government Printing Office, 2000).

31. Ibid.

32. Creagan, *Mayo Clinic Plan.*

33. Charles B. Handy, *The Age of Paradox* (Boston: Harvard Business School Press, 1994).

34. David McClelland, *The Achieving Society* (Princeton, NJ: Van Nostrand, 1967).

35. From a radio interview with Deena Burnett, wife of Tom Burnett and author (with Anthony Giombetti) of *Fighting Back: Living Life Beyond Ourselves: Defining Moments in the Life of an American Hero, Tom Burnett* (Advantage Books, 2006). Tom Burnett was a ringleader of the small group of passengers who fought back against the terrorists on the flight, which crashed into a field in Pennsylvania.

Acknowledgments

Many people have helped me along my purpose path. Some have become stories in the text; for this, I offer my thanks. I also wish to thank all the wise elders, spiritual teachers, and my Inventure Group clients and colleagues who have guided me in matters of purpose.

I wish to express heartfelt gratitude for the vision and encouragement on this project by my inspiring editor, Johanna Vondeling, and the truly on-purpose team at Berrett-Koehler, who support the movement toward a more enlightened world of work. They are an author's dream team. Thanks also to Gaelyn Beal, Sandra Craig, and Detta Penna for their editing and craftsmanship. Their influence is on these pages.

Viktor Frankl and Dick Bolles had a huge influence on my life, career, and writing, and they influenced my whole point of view on purpose. For this inspiration, I am deeply grateful.

And finally, love and gratitude to my wife, Sally. In our relationship I continue to discover the true power of purpose.

Index

About the Author

Richard G. Anderson

Founder and chairman of the Inventure Group, a coaching and consulting firm in Minneapolis, Richard has a worldwide practice working with leaders from organizations such as Ameriprise, Caterpillar, Habitat for Humanity, MetLife, Pfizer, and PriceWaterhouseCoopers.

Richard is consistently rated as one of the top executive educators and coaches in the world. He is ranked by Forbes as one of the Top 5 most respected executive coaches, by Linkage as one of the Top 50 executive coaches, and was called by the Conference Board a "legend in coaching."

As a speaker and seminar leader, he has taught over a hundred thousand executives from fifty corporations worldwide. He is an adjunct faculty member on executive education programs at Duke Corporate Education and a Carlson Executive Education Fellow at the University of Minnesota Carlson School of Management. He is a guest lecturer in Harvard Business School's General Management Program.

Richard is the author of eight books, including three best-sellers, and his work has been translated into twenty-one languages. *Repacking Your Bags* and *The Power of Purpose* are considered classics in the personal development field. *Claiming Your Place at the Fire* and *Something to Live For* have been touted as breakthrough books on positive aging. He is a contributing author to many leading-edge coaching books, including: *Coaching for Leadership, The Art and Practice of Leadership Coaching, Executive Coaching for Results, The Leader of the Future,* and *The Organization of the Future.*

Richard holds a master's degree in counseling and is a nationally certified Master Career Counselor. He is a Senior Fellow at the University of Minnesota's Center for Spirituality and Healing, where he is a founder of the Purpose Project. As a commentator on work/life issues, Richard appears in the *Wall Street Journal,* the *New York Times,* and *USA Today,* and on public television, public radio, and other media sources. Along with his professional pursuits, Richard has led Inventure Expedition walking safaris in Tanzania, East Africa, for twenty-five years.

A pioneer and leader in the field of coaching, Richard is widely recognized for his leading-edge work on helping people discover their calling in work and life. His work received recognition from the Bush Foundation, from which he was awarded a Bush Fellowship to study "purposeful aging." He was named a Distinguished Alumnus by Gustavus Adolphus College and was named to the Hall of Fame at Central High School in Saint Paul. Believing passionately that each of us is born with a purpose, he is dedicated to helping people to discover the power of their own purpose.

Berrett–Koehler
Publishers

Berrett-Koehler is an independent publisher dedicated to an ambitious mission: *Creating a World That Works for All.*

We believe that to truly create a better world, action is needed at all levels—individual, organizational, and societal. At the individual level, our publications help people align their lives with their values and with their aspirations for a better world. At the organizational level, our publications promote progressive leadership and management practices, socially responsible approaches to business, and humane and effective organizations. At the societal level, our publications advance social and economic justice, shared prosperity, sustainability, and new solutions to national and global issues.

A major theme of our publications is "Opening Up New Space." Berrett-Koehler titles challenge conventional thinking, introduce new ideas, and foster positive change. Their common quest is changing the underlying beliefs, mindsets, institutions, and structures that keep generating the same cycles of problems, no matter who our leaders are or what improvement programs we adopt.

We strive to practice what we preach—to operate our publishing company in line with the ideas in our books. At the core of our approach is stewardship, which we define as a deep sense of responsibility to administer the company for the benefit of all of our "stakeholder" groups: authors, customers, employees, investors, service providers, and the communities and environment around us.

We are grateful to the thousands of readers, authors, and other friends of the company who consider themselves to be part of the "BK Community." We hope that you, too, will join us in our mission.

A BK Life Book

This book is part of our BK Life series. BK Life books change people's lives. They help individuals improve their lives in ways that are beneficial for the families, organizations, communities, nations, and world in which they live and work. To find out more, visit **www.bk-life.com.**

Berrett–Koehler
Publishers

A community dedicated to creating
a world that works for all

Visit Our Website: www.bkconnection.com

Read book excerpts, see author videos and Internet movies, read
our authors' blogs, join discussion groups, download book apps, find
out about the BK Affiliate Network, browse subject-area libraries of
books, get special discounts, and more!

Subscribe to Our Free E-Newsletter, the *BK Communiqué*

Be the first to hear about new publications, special discount offers,
exclusive articles, news about bestsellers, and more! Get on the list
for our free e-newsletter by going to **www.bkconnection.com**.

Get Quantity Discounts

Berrett-Koehler books are available at quantity discounts for orders
of ten or more copies. Please call us toll-free at (800) 929-2929 or
email us at bkp.orders@aidcvt.com.

Join the BK Community

BKcommunity.com is a virtual meeting place where people from
around the world can engage with kindred spirits to create a world
that works for all. BKcommunity.com members may create their own
profiles, blog, start and participate in forums and discussion groups,
post photos and videos, answer surveys, announce and register for
upcoming events, and chat with others online in real time. Please join
the conversation!